D1282643

CAPITAL THEORY
AND THE RATE OF RETURN

PROFESSOR DR. F. DE VRIES LECTURES

CAPITAL THEORY AND THE RATE OF RETURN

BY

ROBERT M. SOLOW

Professor of Economics,
Massachusetts Institute of Technology,
Cambridge, Mass.

1964

NORTH-HOLLAND PUBLISHING COMPANY
AMSTERDAM

First Edition 1963
Second Printing 1964

PRINTED IN THE NETHERLANDS

CONTENTS

Professor F. de Vries (1884—1954) became the first professor of economics at the Netherlands School of Economics (Rotterdam), which was founded in 1913. In 1945 he accepted an offer of the University of Amsterdam to teach economics in its Faculty of Law. On the occasion of his 70th birthday, May 2, 1954 his pupils created the Prof. F. de Vries Foundation to honour a most influential teacher and a scholar of outstanding theoretical and practical wisdom.

The aim of the foundation is regularly to invite prominent economists from abroad for a series of lectures on theoretical subjects, as a stimulus to theoretical work in economics in the Netherlands.

INTRODUCTION

Professor Robert M. Solow took his Ph. D. degree at Harvard University in 1951. From 1950 to 1954 he was Assistant Professor, from 1954–1958 Associate Professor and since 1958 he is full Professor at the Massachusetts Institute of Technology. From 1961–1962 he was Senior Economist at the Council of Economic Advisers and Head of the U.S. Delegation to the O.E.C.D. Working Party on Policies for the Promotion of Economic Growth. Currently Professor Solow is Vice-President of the Econometric Society, the world organization of econometrists, implying that he will be its President in 1964.

Professor Solow is widely known for his penetrating work, both theoretical and empirical, in econometrics and more particularly in the fields of production functions and economic development. Very well versed in the mathematical treatment of economics he is the author or co-author of a number of thorough theoretical studies on these subjects, including their linear programming applications. Professor Solow, however, also made some substantial contributions to the statistical testing of production functions, implying research on the contribution made by technological development to productivity.

The F. de Vries Foundation feels honoured to be able to publish these lectures of a distinguished scholar.

J. Tinbergen.

PREFACE

This series of volumes stands as a permanent memorial to Professor F. de Vries. I would like to dedicate these lectures more particularly to the memory of Leendert M. Koyck, who died so suddenly and so recently. I did not know Leen Koyck very well; we spent a happy summer in Salzburg in 1948 and I had not seen him since. But we corresponded occasionally, followed each other's work and sometimes worked at the same subject: distributed lags a few years ago, and more recently the general subject of these lectures. I had looked forward to seeing him again in Rotterdam. Economists everywhere will share my sense of loss.

These lectures are printed as they were written, for oral delivery. There are no detailed footnotes, but I have included a brief list of references to the recent literature which will reveal some of my intellectual debts. My friend and colleague Paul Samuelson read the first draft and contributed many valuable comments. We have collaborated in this field for so long that it is impossible for me to say whether any given idea originated with him, with me, or in between. Mrs. Charlotte Phelps did yeowoman work with the computations. Miss Laura Heath typed and retyped the manuscript at a busy time with no loss of skill or good humor.

It is a pleasure to thank Professor J. Tinbergen, Professor H. Lambers, Mrs. M. 't Hooft and my other friends at the Netherlands School of Economics for the hospitality that made our stay in the Netherlands so enjoyable.

CHAPTER I

CAPITAL AND THE RATE OF RETURN

Introduction

In beginning the first series of de Vries Lectures 8 years ago, Professor James Meade remarked that it might seem foolhardy for an Englishman to come to Holland to lecture about customs unions. He could have gone a step further: it is a little superfluous for any foreigner to come to Rotterdam to lecture about economics at all. I feel a bit like a 17th century New England smuggler lecturing on seamanship to Admiral Tromp. The trade in economics nowadays is as much the other way: we send our young men to Rotterdam to learn, not our middle-aged professors to teach. Indeed, some of our best middle-aged professors are named Koopmans and Houthakker! I suppose the logic of the situation is that I am not an import at all; I am to be processed and re-exported, like cocoa beans.

In any case, I am a foreigner come for a 'series of lectures on theoretical subjects'. The particular theoretical subject I have chosen is the theory of capital, especially in its relation to economic growth.

Before I settle down to my business, however, I would like to say something about economic theory in general. Economics, like physics or astronomy I imagine, has a body of fairly simple low-powered theory and a body of rather fancy high-powered theory. But there is a subtle difference between economics and physical science. In physics, so far as an outsider can judge, you have to master the simple theory in order to gain access to the fancy theory; and many spectacular practical achievements seem to have come from the fancy theory. In economics, things are different. I like a man to have mastered the fancy theory before I trust him with the simple theory. The practical utility of economics comes not primarily from its high-powered frontier, but from fairly low-powered reasoning. (I think this occurs not for any intrinsic reason, but because the data are not available to give precision to high-powered theory. And in addition, it often turns out that the high-powered theory of today is the low-powered theory of tomorrow). But the moral is not that we can dispense with high-powered economics, if only because high-powered economics seems to be such an excellent school for the skillful use of low-powered economics. The Tinbergen of 1935 was an indispensable preparation for the Tinbergen of today, indeed for all of us today. And what the Theil of today is a preparation for, we can only guess.

I bring this up now in part to assure you that I intend to discuss capital theory in a low-powered way. My object is to arrive—before the end of the third lecture—at a few rough empirical statements about the relation between capital accumulation and economic growth in industrial countries today. The only available theoretical foundation for such statements is a modernized version of neo-classical or late-Wicksellian capital theory. Since much controversy still swirls about this subject, I think I should begin by stating clearly what seems to me to be still valid and viable in the neo-neo-classical theory of capital. I hope to do that in this lecture.

This afternoon I want to discuss how the theory needs to be refined and modified to deal with technological progress. And finally, tomorrow I would like to consider the relation between saving and investment and the long-run growth of productive capacity.

The Place of Capital Theory in Economics

The theory of capital has been a subject of controversy among economists at least since Torrens attacked Ricardo's theory of value in 1818. Most of the neo-classical theoretical structure has by now been consigned more or less definitely either to orthodoxy or to error. But the status of capital theory is still unsettled. A more learned reader of the literature than I could probably show that the capital theory pot has been simmering steadily ever since Ricardo's chapter on Machinery. At intervals it has boiled over on a heroic scale: in the polemics between Böhm-Bawerk and J. B. Clark in the 1890's, between Hayek and Knight—going over much the same ground—in the 1920's and 1930's, and between Mrs. Joan Robinson and almost everyone else outside of Cambridge, England in the present. Between his famous Econometrica article of 1937 and his latest work, Nicholas Kaldor appears in some respects to have switched sides; I am afraid I prefer early Kaldor to late.

It seems that some of the same questions that were debated in the 19th century, for example, how should 'capital' be measured, remain matters of contention today. I speak diffidently about this because I find the earlier discussions terribly confusing and occasionally incomprehensible to a contemporary economist. Indeed, I suppose I should confess I sometimes feel much the same way about the current discussion even though—even when—I take part in it myself. This is a matter of some significance, because when a theoretical question remains debatable after 80 years there is a presumption that the question is badly posed—or very deep indeed. I believe that the question of the measurement of 'capital' is badly posed, and I hope I can bring you around to my point of view.

One can legitimately wonder why capital theory lends itself so easily to violent, unproductive, and confused controversy. I think there are two reasons for this, one intrinsic to the subject and one incidental, or at least intellectually incidental. Let me mention the incidental reason first, because we will not have to return to it. It is an ideological reason. One of the perennial questions of 19th century capital theory was: 'Why is the interest rate positive?' Obviously, this is only a hair's breadth from asking: 'Why do capitalists earn an income, and is it just that they should do so?' In one sense 19th century capital theory had the social function of providing an ideological justification for profit. I hope you realize that this remark by itself in no way impugns the motives of individual economists and says nothing at all about the scientific validity of their doctrines. But it says something (not everything) about their peculiar terminology and the resistance it sometimes arouses.

Workers get paid for working; what do capitalists get paid for? For 'waiting' while roundabout processes of production percolate, or for 'abstaining' from some current consumption in favor of replacing or augmenting the stock of capital and maintaining or increasing future consumption. Since so much of the 'waiting' gets done in expensive automobiles and luxurious resorts, while the 'abstinence' excites little sympathy in an even slightly cynical observer, the whole apparatus begins to look like a transparent verbal trick. (Indeed, I think 'abstinence' is an even more repulsive way of putting it than 'waiting', though if one could strip away the moral or moralistic overtones, I think it is an economically more useful description.) But even so, there is no excuse for economists to lose the concept in their resentment at the language. One of the elegant showpieces of economics is its analysis of the resource-allocation implications of a system of prices or shadow prices. We have learned to free this analysis of ethical overtones. All that is necessary in capital theory is to draw a conceptual distinction between the imputed return to capital and the income of capitalists. Here, as elsewhere in economics, but with rather more irony here, the best way of understanding the economics of capitalism may be to think about a socialist economy.

There is also an intrinsic reason for the controversial character of capital theory: it is very complicated and very difficult. I think the Austrian school overdid the identification of capital itself (and capital theory) with time—it was an inspired simplification that didn't work—but the need for a theory of capital does arise only when we try to take account of production processes which involve time in some essential way. I say *some* essential way: the point is that there are many essential ways in which time may enter the production process. Adding the time dimension opens up a bewildering variety of partial models of production, of theories which take careful account of some aspect of inter-

11

temporal life only at the expense of neglecting other aspects. What pass for different theories of capital often turn out to be simply idealizations of different aspects of the role of time in production. And some of the violent polemics arise because one economist persists in thinking about grape juice while another thinks about machinery.

A man from Mars reading the literature on capital theory would be inclined sometimes to think that capital consists mainly of stocks of consumer goods to maintain workers until their output can be sold; sometimes he would think that the earth is given over to the maturing of wine and the growing of trees, so that capital consists largely of goods in process; sometimes he would realize that most of what we think of as capital consists of durable assets like buildings and machinery, or what we call fixed capital. He would perhaps wonder why Wicksell, in the course of a careful analysis of a model with fixed capital in the form of axes, did not pay any attention to the age of the trees being cut down (though he had done so 30 years earlier), whereas Böhm-Bawerk, who seemed to be thinking mainly about the age at which trees should be cut down, seemed to worry too little about the implement to be used in felling them. He would be a little uncertain whether gestation periods matter a lot or not, whether production is like making elephants or making mosquitoes. The truth, of course, is that all these aspects of capitalistic production are important, that it is useless to try to represent all of them by any one of them, and extraordinarily complicated to deal simultaneously with them all.

If this complexity of structure were all that stood between

us and a satisfactory theory of capital, it would be nothing that a team from the Netherlands School of Economics and the Massachusetts Institute of Technology could not lick in a few years of hard work. But there is a further fundamental difficulty that bedevils even uncomplicated models. Capital problems are inevitably bound up with questions of uncertainty, limited foresight, and reactions to the unexpected. One must admit that economics has barely scratched the surface here. Yet without a satisfactory account of behavior under uncertainty we cannot have a complete theory of capital.

Seen from this rather modest point of view, many of the heated controversies of both past and present seem to lose point. It does not really matter whether the rate of interest is a measure of the marginal productivity of 'time' or the marginal productivity of 'capital', or the marginal productivity of any 'thing', since interest will clearly enter in different ways in production processes of quite different technological character. It does not really matter whether the period of production in processes involving fixed capital is finite or infinite, or even whether it can be well defined at all, because the period of production is a concept designed to help analyze production involving predominantly circulating capital, and one would not expect it to be especially helpful in dealing with fixed capital. It does not really matter whether 'capital' is a primary factor of production, nor is it especially important to ask how 'capital' is to be measured. For there is no reason to suppose that any single object called 'capital' can be defined to sum up in one number a whole range of facts about time lags, gestation periods, inventories of materials, goods in process, and finished commodities, old and new machines and buildings of varying durability, and more or less permanent improvements to land. Only someone who is naively identifying all the many aspects of capitalistic production with one of them, it does not matter which, would believe that the theory can be summed up by defining something called 'capital' and calling the interest rate the marginal productivity of 'it'.

But then what is the proper scope of capital theory, and on what real problems can it throw light?

There is a highbrow answer to this question and a lowbrow one. The highbrow answer is that the theory of capital is after all just a part of the fundamentally microeconomic theory of the allocation of resources, necessary to allow for the fact that commodities can be transformed into other commodities over time. Just as the theory of resource allocation has as its 'dual' a theory of competitive pricing, so the theory of capital has as its 'dual' a theory of intertemporal pricing involving rentals, interest rates, present values and the like. In both cases, a complete price theory is also a theory of distribution among factors of production, if not among persons.

The lowbrow answer, I suppose, is that theory is supposed to help us understand real problems, and the real problems that cannot be understood without capital-theoretic notions are those connected with saving and investment. Therefore the proper scope of capital theory is the elucidation of the causes and consequences of acts of saving and investment. Where the highbrow approach tends to be technical, disaggregated, and exact, the lowbrow view tends to be pecuniary, aggregative, and approximate.

A middlebrow like myself sees virtue in each of these ways of looking at capital theory. I am personally attracted by what I have described as the lowbrow view of the function of capital theory. But as so often happens, I think the highbrow view offers indispensable help in achieving the lowbrow objective. In particular, the suggestion that capital theory is an extension of ordinary resource allocation and price theory reminds one that modern microeconomics has two aspects which might be called the descriptive and the technocratic or the positive and the normative. Price theory began as an idealized description of how resources are allocated and income distributed in a competitive capitalist economy. But further analysis, as you know, uncovered something remarkable: if you try to answer not that descriptive question but the normative or technocratic one of how scarce resources should be allocated by a society anxious to avoid waste, you rediscover the same theory in the guise of shadow prices or efficiency prices. This line of thought originated a long time ago, but culminates in the modern work on linear and nonlinear programming and in the paradox that the theory of perfectly-competitive capitalism is in many respects the theory of a planned or socialist economy.

Capital theory, too, has a technocratic and a descriptive side. I believe that the easiest and safest route to a simple but rigorous view of the subject is to begin technocratically. By asking planning questions, allocation questions, we can, as I hope to show, dodge many embarrassing questions of definition and their ideological overtones. The fundamental difficulty of uncertainty cannot really be dodged; and since it cannot be faced, it must simply be ignored. If I am right in

15

thinking that much empty controversy arises because the questions asked are pointless, then the planning point of view may be a useful one. A planning question, after all, is likely to have an answer. Of course, with this gain in clarity comes a certain risk. It may be claimed that a capital theory erected on planning grounds has no relevance to the actual behavior of any real capitalist economy. That argument has often been made, with considerable success, against static competitive price theory. Capital theory is unlikely to be immune to the same complaint. But if we fail in this way to explain the actual distribution of income between profits and wages, we may yet be able to answer the lowbrow question about the consequences, if not the causes, of saving and investment decisions.

The Rate of Return on Investment

Thinking about saving and investment from this technocratic point of view has convinced me that the central concept in capital theory should be *the rate of return on investment.* In short, we really want a theory of interest rates, not a theory of capital. I do not believe that this shift of emphasis makes the theory of capital easy; but I do believe that concentrating on the rate of return leads to clarity of though, while concentrating on 'time', or 'capital', or the 'marginal productivity of capital', or the 'capital-output ratio' has led to confusion. It seems to me that almost any important planning question we wish to ask about the saving-investment process has an unambiguous if perhaps approximate answer in terms of rates of return, whereas the answers sometimes given in terms of marginal products of capital and capital-output ratios are sometimes right, sometimes wrong, and often misleading. I suppose that my point of view could be described as a modern amalgamation of Wicksell and Irving Fisher.

I must emphasize that I am not now identifying the rate of return on investment with the rate of profit or the observed market rate of interest or any form of income receipt in a capitalist economy. That can perhaps sometimes be done, but it is in any case part of the descriptive theory. My technocratic notion of the rate of return on investment must be entirely independent of the institutional arrangements of the economy. I had better suggest such a definition in fairly general terms; later I shall show how the general definition works in the context of particular models.

Imagine an economy which produces a single consumer good (which may be a fixed-weight bundle of various elementary consumer goods) according to any reasonably well-behaved technology. There may be any number of primary factors of production, from natural resource deposits to labor of different quality and skill characteristics. I assume that production makes use of physical capital goods which are themselves produced—buildings, machines, inventories; in addition, the production of the consumer good and some or all of the capital goods may involve delay periods of various lengths, fixed or variable. One could hardly ask for more freedom in describing the techniques of production. Now imagine any arbitrary planned allocation of resources in this economy for the current year. By an allocation of resources I mean a complete specification of productive activities for the period: how much of the consumer good is to be produced, with what resources, capital goods, and labor services;

17

how much of what kinds of capital goods are to be produced, and with what inputs. All I ask of this arbitrary allocation is that it be efficient in the usual sense that, with the labor, resources, and capital goods available, it would not be possible to produce a bundle of capital and consumer goods providing more of some useful things without providing less of others. Efficiency implies, among other things, that there is no 'non-structural' unemployment of labor or other primary resources, or of productive capacity.

The planning authority in this economy could, and should, at least contemplate neighboring efficient resource allocations which produce a little less of the consumer good, *i.e.* which involve a little more saving, than the planned one. Because all the allocations considered are efficient, those which produce less consumption must also produce more of at least some kinds of capital goods. To be specific, consider all allocations which yield, say, h units less of current consumption than the planned allocation (where h is a small number). Now the planning authority must think ahead. If it adopts the planned allocation for the current period, the society will be left with certain supplies of primary factors and stocks of capital goods in the next period, and thus with a collection of possible allocations for the next period. Let the planning authority decide which one it will in fact choose from the collection. Call C_0 the planned consumption for the current period and C_1 the planned consumption for the next period. At the end of the next period the economy will possess certain productive capacities and potentials for periods 2, 3, and later.

Now return to those possible current allocations which

18

yield $C_0 - h$ in current consumption and which leave, presumably, generally more capacity available for the next period. For each of these alternative current allocations, select a next-period allocation which would send the economy on into period 2 with the same productive capacities and potentials as the planned current and next allocations (or with *equivalent* capacities and potentials, in the sense that any stream of consumption producible by one stock of capital and resources is producible by the other). Suppose that such a next-period allocation yields next-period consumption of $C_1 + k$. Presumably k will be positive, since the alternative allocation yields more current saving and therefore more next-period capacity than the planned allocation; in any case k cannot be negative for all alternative allocations, unless the economy is already over-saturated with capital goods. Finally, among all the alternative current and next-period allocations allowing $C_0 - h$ consumption in the current period and equivalent potentials for period 2 and later, find the one which yields the largest k, the largest gain in next-period consumption over the planned pair of allocations. Thus by sacrificing h units of consumption in the present, society can earn an extra consumption of k units next period and suffer no ill effects thereafter. In such a case I would of course define the one-period rate of return on investment as $(k - h)/h = k/h - 1$. This is perfectly natural usage. If by saving an extra $ 1.00 of consumption this year society can enjoy at most $ 1.10 of consumption next year without endangering its later prospects, then one would certainly want to say that society has earned 10 per cent on its investment.

19

Before I go further, let me make two fairly obvious remarks. First, the technocratic planning authority could just as well contemplate an increase in current consumption which would have to be paid for by a decrease in next-period consumption, in order to leave more distant future prospects undamaged. In that case h and k would both be negative and the one-period rate of return could be calculated exactly as before. If the technology is very smooth, then the rates of return for increases and decreases in saving will be approximately the same, and will draw closer together as h gets smaller. But even in quite well-behaved technologies of the not-so-smooth linear-programming type, the upward and downward rates of return can differ even for very small h. If the technology exhibits constant returns to scale and enough diminishing returns, the rate of return for decreases in saving will exceed that for increases in saving, if they differ at all.

Second, my restriction to a consumption bundle of unchanging composition is only an expository simplification. If there are many consumption goods, then the planned current allocation, since it is efficient, implies certain marginal rates of transformation among them. (If the allocation is Pareto-optimal with respect to the preferences of citizens or technocrats then these rates of transformation will coincide with marginal rates of substitution in consumption). For small changes in saving, it is adequate to calculate the rate of return at the margin in terms of any one consumer good or subtractions and additions of small bundles of consumer goods of arbitrary composition. This is so for the same reason that, in static production theory, when costs are being

20

minimized, marginal labor costs equal marginal material costs equal marginal equipment costs equal marginal costs no matter how a small increment in output is obtained. In non-smooth technologies the situation will not be so simple.

The concept discussed so far is clearly a one-period or short-run rate of return; it is as if the economy could deposit consumption goods in a bank account and draw them out, with interest, at the end of the year. The rate of return, as I have defined it, is the rate of interest paid by the bank on one-year deposits—only the bank is really the complete collection of capital-using production processes in the economy. (In a technology with corners and jumps, the interest earned on an extra deposit may differ from the interest lost on an extra withdrawal, and the difference may not be small. There is nothing ambiguous in such a situation, but it is more complicated to describe. One should not slay the theoretical messenger for bringing the bad news that the world is complicated.)

There is a case for saying that these one-period rates of return are the fundamental ones because, in a highly-developed and complex growing economy, saving-investment decisions come up for reconsideration every period and can easily be changed or even undone; so that even a long and complicated investment program can probably be duplicated by a series of cleverly-chosen short-term programs. Nevertheless, the planning authority may, sometimes by choice, sometimes by technological necessity, compare the consumption stream yielded by the planned allocation with alternatives stretching over more than two periods. The choice of time profiles for enjoying the fruits of a current increment to saving is uncomfortably wide. For some of them it is easy to define a rate of return to the initial act of saving-investment. If the alternative is to save an extra h units of consumption now, hold consumption next period at the same level C_1 as in the planned allocation, consume all that is possible in the period after—$C_2' = C_2 + k$—under the constraint that C_3, C_4 ... must ever after be at their levels in the trial planned allocation, then the average rate of return per period on this two-year investment is defined by $k/h = (1 + r_{t2})^2$. Quite similarly, if the authority should decide to save now, go back to planned consumption levels for $n - 1$ periods, and then splurge everything in the n'th period (subject to the same guarantee about subsequent periods), and if C_n were the originally-planned n'th period consumption and C_n' the most that can be consumed under the alternative plans, then the average n-period rate of return must be the solution of $(C_n' - C_n)/(C_0 - C_0') = (1 + r_{tn})^n$. As usual, I am assuming $C_0 - C_0'$ to be small.

There is one other easy case—in principle at least. The planning authority could choose to sacrifice an extra h units of consumption and then so arrange things as to add a constant amount to each period's previously planned consumption, in perpetuity. Thus we have $C_0' = C_0 - h$, $C_1' = C_1 + p$, $C_2' = C_2 + p$, etc. If p is the largest such perpetual increment to consumption that can be maintained, it is natural to describe p/h as the average rate of return in perpetuity. I will work out such a calculation for a particular model later.

More complicated time profiles are more difficult to summarize in a single rate of return per period. It is tempting to take an arbitrary stream of algebraic increments to the

22

originally planned consumption stream, some positive, some negative, and find the rate of interest that equates its present value to the current saving making it possible; this is in effect simply a marginal efficiency of investment or internal rate of return. It is, of course, open to the difficulty that if there are negative as well as positive changes in planned consumption, then there may be more than one marginal efficiency of investment for a single alternative consumption program. It is open to the much more serious objection that it often leads to incorrect decisions. The best procedure is to get along without internal rates. The short-run, technologically-defined rates of return are the basic material and all that is necessary can be constructed from them. They need not be averaged into some over-all figure.

This difficulty with complicated multi-period consumption programs gets even deeper when one considers economies in which technological progress is occurring, as I shall do in the next lecture. Even without technological change, the nature of the problem is illustrated by the fact that as I have defined it even the one-period rate of return on investment depends (perhaps sensitively, perhaps not) on the level of consumption for this period and the next period as they appear in the original plan. *A fortiori*, for longer periods the stream of returns from a marginal act of saving-investment now will depend on what had been planned for the future anyway. This dependence merely reflects the fact that I am considering small variations around some pre-existing situation, as is always done in static economics (and that restriction is not strictly necessary except for shadow-price interpretations). But since time plays a role in my problem, I must specify the base situation, from which possible displacements occur, in full detail.

This is a problem of execution, not of principle, and I do not think it either surprising or terribly important. In the first place, it clearly does not signify that the planning problem has no solution. The abstract technocrat or planner need never worry about helpful little constructs like the rate of return on investment. He need 'only' consider all possible future time profiles for the economy emanating from the current state of affairs, eliminate te obviously inefficiente ons,o and choose the best (the most preferred) out of the ones remaining. There is no reason on earth to expect this procedure in full generality to reduce to the business of calculating a bunch of rates of return and a bunch of rates of time preference and comparing the two bunches. But the middle-brow economist may want to have some such routine because a simplified model yielding an approximate result may be good enough for him. (As to the thin line between simplified and over-simplified models, I can do no better than quote the English philosopher J. L. Austin: '... we must at all costs avoid over-simplification, which one might be tempted to call the occupational disease of philosophers if it were not their occupation'.)

This is the role the special notion of the stationary state played in 19th century capital theory. It provided a simple and convenient class of base situations from which one could easily calculate possible displacements: either from one stationary state to a neighboring one, or from a stationary state to a slight deviation and then back to the same stationary state. In the modern mood we are more likely to take as our base situations the class of states of balanced growth at the natural rate of growth, and go through the same routine of considering small displacements. My guess is that for most of the problems likely to confront the general economist some natural comparison will present itself. I have already mentioned the likelihood that in a complex modern economy the one-period return is likely to be specially important because decisions regenerate themselves fairly quickly. These two advantages taken together suggest to me that for many macroeconomic problems in capital theory it is enough to look at, say, the one-year rate h return on investment, thef rate of return in perpetuity, and perhaps a ten-year rate of return in between.

I have been suggesting that the rate of return on acts of saving and investment is a good organizing concept for middlebrow capital theory. One of the advantages of looking at capital theory this way is that one automatically dodges most or all of the real or imaginary 'problems' that have beset this branch of economics for so long. In particular, to calculate the rate of return in my sense requires no measurement of the stock of 'capital'. What is more, a careful person will see that the whole process can be described without even mentioning the word 'capital'. If there are concrete capital goods, or inventories, or delay periods, these will all of course affect the rate at which bundles of current consumption goods can be transformed into bundles of future consumption goods. But unless it is a natural thing to do under the technological circumstances, there is no need to identify or measure a stock of generalized capital. If the economy throws up market prices or if the process of analysis yields some kind of efficiency prices, then there is no harm in adding up various value sums which may correspond to the market (or other) value of the stock of capital goods. But such value sums are not 'capital' in the sense of something that belongs in a production function and has a marginal product. Similarly, it may turn out in theory that the rate of return on investment is equal to the rate of interest, defined as the ratio of the value of certain flows of goods to the value of the stock of capital goods. But then again, it may not. In any case all of this begins to belong to the descriptive theory of capital. I am content with the point that the problem of measuring 'capital' simply does not arise in my way of looking at the theory.

It is also said sometimes, that neo-classical capital theory must rest on such obviously absurd assumptions as that capital goods are 'malleable' in the sense that one kind of machine can be instantaneously and costlessly transformed into any other kind or that specific capital goods can be substituted smoothly for labor and other inputs in the production of homogeneous output. The idea is that 'malleability' is necessary in order that there be something called 'capital' to calculate the marginal productivity of, and 'smooth substitutability' is necessary in order to calculate the marginal productivity of 'it'. I think you can see that both of these contentions are wrong. Extreme assumptions like malleability and smooth substitutability make neo-classical capital theory easier (whether they give badly distorted conclusions is hard to say); but they are not essential to it. To the extent that neo-classical capital theory can be built around the rate of return concept—including the accompanying efficiency-price

26

theory and the possible identification with market prices and interest rates—it can accomodate fixity of form and proportions both.

The kernel of useful truth in the John Bates Clark picture of capital as a kind of jelly that transforms itself over time is that indeed, over time, something like this does happen as capital goods wear out and are replaced by different capital goods. The rigorous counterpart of this process is this: when capital goods are highly specific there may be sudden jumps in one-period rates of return relating to the present and near future. But as one looks further and further into the future the substitution possibilities become smoother and smoother and rates of return narrow down.

These are negative advantages of thinking in terms of the rate of return. I think there are positive advantages too. For rational planning at the microeconomic level, whether within a business firm or a government agency concerned with particular investment projects, admittedly there is no substitute for detailed knowledge of technical and economic interrelations. But at a more macroeconomic stage there appears to be no substitute for summary statistics. It seems to me that the needs of high-order decision-making, about such things as the overall rate of consumption and the choice among broad areas of investment, are best served by information cast in the form of rates of return. The only way one can make sense of the capital-output ratios or incremental capital-output ratios or other such numbers that occasionally crop up, is to suppose that they are meant as crude approximations to one or another of the social rates of return on investment. If that is so, there are many reasons to believe

27

that they are very crude approximations indeed, and economists have a responsibility to do better. One only has to ask whether rational saving-investment decisions can be independent of the durability of the structures and equipment involved or of the complementary inputs of labor and materials required. In all cases when the answer is no—that is, in all cases—the rate of return is a useful indicator of the choices facing society, while capital-output ratios are not.

(I should also add that a technocratic theory of real capital emphasizing the return on investment has the advantage of linking up with contemporary efforts to refine the descriptive theory of asset preferences and monetary macro-dynamics. In particular, James Tobin's recent work turns on the key notion of the rate of return required to induce the public to hold willingly the volume of real capital in existence at the moment as well as the increments contributed by current saving. He is concerned with how this required rate depends on the volume of financial assets in the portfolios of the public and on the actions of the fiscal and monetary authorities. I am concerned with the rate of return the stock of real capital goods is able to provide and how it depends on changes in technology and the cumulation of past saving. The two parts of the theory fit together nicely.)

Some Examples

I must now give some examples, not yet from different factual situations but from different models or theoretical situations, postponing discussion of technical progress until later.

The most familiar model is the one most often criticized.

Consider an economy producing one all-purpose commodity which can be consumed or else used as a capital good and combined with labor in continuously variable proportions to produce more of itself. Suppose that a fixed fraction of the stock of the commodity evaporates or wears out each year, independent of age. (This is a very important simplifying assumption. Without it, the stream of production possibilities implicit in the stock depends not only on its size but on its age distribution. Any variation in the rate of investment will disturb the age distribution and it may take a long time to restore it or a long computation to verify whether two slightly different stocks of capital actually convey equivalent production possibilities.)

At time zero, the economy is endowed with a stock of the all-purpose commodity in the amount S_0; the planning authorities have command over L_0 man-years of labor. Together these permit an output $F(S_0, L_0) = Q_0$, where $F(S_0, L_0)$ is a standard smooth textbook production function. Q_0 can be divided up arbitrarily into consumption C_0 and gross investment I_0, so that $Q_0 = C_0 + I_0$. If this is what the technocrats plan, then in the next period they will dispose of a stock $S_1 = (1-d)S_0 + I^0$ where d is de rate of mortality on existing capital. They will also have available L_1 man-years of labor, assumed exogenous. They can therefore choose $C_1 + I_1 = Q_1 = F(S_1, L_1)$ and go into period 2 with $S_2 = (1-d)S_1 + I_1 = (1-d)^2 S_0 + (1-d)I_0 + I_1$.

Now suppose we contemplate reducing C_0 to $C_0' = C_0 - h$. In period 1, the available stock becomes $S_1' = S_1 + h$ and total output rises to $F(S_1 + h, L_1) = Q_1 + hF_1(S_1, L_1)$ where $F_1(S_1, L_1)$ is of course the marginal gross productivity of capital with the size of stock and labor force ruling in period 1 under the base plan. (This model is of course over-simplified, but within it I can speak without embarrassment of the marginal productivity of capital.) Now the rules of the game require us (or the planners) to leave a stock equal to S_2 in period 2. What is the largest consumption C_1' which will permit that? One can easily work it out arithmetically: $S_2 = (1 - d) S_1 + Q_1 - C_1 = (1 - d) S_1' + I_1' = (1 - d) (S_1 h) + Q_1 + hF_1 - C_1'$, so that $C_1' = C_1 + h (1-d) + hF_1$. Or else one can simply say that the extra consumption permitted in period 1 is the extra output produced plus the extra bit of capital saved in period 0, after allowance for that part which has evaporated. The extra consumption is thus $h (1-d+F_1)$, and the one-period rate of return is $h(1 - d + F_1)/h - 1 = F_1(S_1, L_1) - d$. It is, therefore, the net marginal product of capital in period 1, which will come as no surprise to anyone.

For a second example I choose a highly simplified model in which the technology permits no *direct* subsitution between labor and capital. It seems to me that in real life the appropriate assumption is that something like fixed technical coefficients rule in the short run and a fairly wide range of substitutability rules in the long run. But my object now is simply to show by example that the rate of return on investment does not depend for its existence and meaning on the possibility of defining 'marginal productivities' or having smoothly variable proportions between the factors of production. The model is due to David Worswick.

Consider an economy producing a single consumer good or bundle of consumer goods. There are two known techniques for producing the consumer good. One is a primitive handicraft method, according to which one man working for one year can produce b units of consumables. The second technique uses machines: it takes n men to operate one machine, and together they can produce nc units of consumables in a year. Machines in turn are produced by labor alone. (This assumption greatly simplifies the algebraic calculations I must make without being in the least necessary to my argument). A crew of m men working for a year can produce one machine. I shall assume that a fraction d of all machines in existence disappear by depreciation at the end of the year, while the remaining $(1-d)$ survive into the next period.

Suppose the total supply of labor is stationary. The technocrats dispose of L workers, L_M of whom are engaged in making machines, L_c in using machines to manufacture consumer goods, and L_h in producing consumer goods by hand. Thus $L_M + L_c + L_h = L$. Suppose for definiteness and simplicity that plans call for this division not to change. Let M be the stock of machines in existence. If this stock is to be maintained, the annual output of machines must be dM, and therefore $L_M = dmM$. Since all M machines are used to produce consumer goods, we have that $L_c = nM$. Finally, if C is the annual output of consumer goods, $C = ncM + bL_h = cL_c + bL_h$.

Now let the planning authority consider the sacrifice of some present consumption for future consumption. The natural, indeed the only sensible, way to bring this about is to transfer some labor from the hand production of consumer goods to the hand production of machines. The main function of the hand-production-of-consumables sector in this model is to provide a reservoir of labor that can be transferred to machine production. Suppose we contemplate transferring one worker. Then C will be reduced by b units, *i.e.* the act of saving consists of foregoing the b units of consumables that worker could have produced. The transferred worker will instead produce $1/m$ machines. And so in the next period the stock of machines will be increased to $M + (1/m)$.

The question is: how much extra consumption is now possible in the following period, with the understanding that at the end of the period the stock of machines must be what it would have been if this extra bit of saving had never occurred? The answer is perfectly straightforward. The stock of machines will diminish by depreciation to $(1 - d)$ $(M + 1/m)$. To restore it at the end of the period to its stationary level M requires production of $dM - (1-d)/m$ machines, and therefore the work of $dmM - (1-d)$ men. On the other hand, to operate the $M + 1$ m machines requires $nM + n/m$ men. The number of men left now to produce consumer goods by hand is $L - dmM + (1 - d) - nM - n/m$. This exceeds the old number of men in this industry by $(1-d) - n/m$, which may be positive or negative. In any case the total output of consumer goods in this second period exceeds what it would have been under the old plan by $(nc/m) + b [(1 - d) - n/m]$. Since the amount of consumption initially sacrificed is b, the rate of return is $nc/mb - n/m - d = (n/m) [(c/b) - 1] - d$ according to the formula I gave earlier.

In this case it is easy to calculate the rate of return in perpetuity, and I do so to illustrate that under stationary

32

conditions the one-period and perpetual rates of return (and all intermediate ones) are the same. The story goes just as before except that to maintain the stock of machines at the new level $M + 1/m$ requires that annual production of machines rise by d/m, which requires the permanent addition of d men to the machine-building sector. The machine-using sector requires n/m new operatives from now on. They produce a flow of consumables higher by nc/m than it used to be. But against this must be written off the $b(d + n/m)$ in output from the handworking sector that is permanently lost because some manpower must be permanently transferred to the replacing and operating of new machines. Thus for its initial sacrifice of b units of consumption, society realizes a perpetual flow of $nc/m - b \ (d + n/m)$ units of consumables. The rate of return is thus $nc/mb - n/m - d$, just as it was before.

In the first, wholly neo-classical, model the rate of return equals the marginal productivity of capital and it hardly seemes worthwhile to point out the connection with the theory of a market economy: in a perfect capital market the only possible equilibrium interest rate is one equal to the rate of return on investment. In this second model precisely the same thing is true: in competitive equilibrium, the rate of interest must equal the rate of return on investment. The nc units of consumer goods produced by one machine and n men must cover the wages of the n men, depreciation on the machine, and profit or interest on the value of the machine. Thus $nc = wn + wm \ (d + r)$ where now w is the wage in consumer goods, r is the unknown rate of interest, and wm is clearly the amount of 'capital value' tied up in a machine. But the wage in consumables is fixed at b, because one worker can produce b units of consumables unassisted in the handicraft sector; whatever the institutional character of the economy, the opportunity cost of adding one unit of labor to the machine-building-and-using sectors is clearly b units of consumer goods as long as anyone is employed in the handicraft sector. But then $nc = bn + bm\,(d+r)$, which implies $r = nc/bm - d - n/m$. Thus even here, with no marginal productivities defined, the only possible equilibrium interest rate is the rate of return on investment.

I could continue with more complicated and more interesting models of production: distinguishing the investment goods sector and the consumption goods sector, introducing machines to make machines, or perhaps various kinds of machines, some more 'mechanized' than others, allowing for time lags between input and output, considering initial situations which are not stationary. The result is always pretty much the same. Without any dubious 'measurement of capital', within whatever technological assumptions instinct and observation lead one to make, it is possible to pose and to answer what I have claimed to be the central question of capital theory. What is the payoff to society from an extra bit of saving transformed efficiently into capital formation?

This is more than a safe question to ask; it is an important one. I don't see how a nation can have a rational investment policy until it has found approximate answers to such questions as these: what is the social rate of return to saving? Is there a substantial gap between the private and social returns to saving and investment? What are the long-run consequences of long-term thrift? For answers which will be relevant to modern economic conditions, the first necessity is to see whether this view of capital theory can be extended to cover situations in which technological progress is occurring. I propose to turn to that problem in the next lecture.

CHAPTER II

THE RATE OF RETURN AND TECHNICAL PROGRESS

Introduction

I tried in the preceding lecture to indicate how the theory of capital can be developed in a way that is free of many of those 'fundamental' criticisms about the measurement of 'capital', the definition of the 'period of production', and others which have occupied so much discussion. The trick is to concentrate on the consequences of decisions about saving and investment, and this in turn suggests the wisdom of carrying on the analysis in terms of the rate of return on investment, a dimensionless number (per unit of time) and one which will have meaning no matter how we choose to idealize the process of capitalistic production in our models. Nor does this way of looking at capital theory require us to abandon such vague but plausible notions as the belief that 'capital-deepening' or increases in capital intensity lead to decreases in interest rates (or vice versa). But I would rephrase the statement to say, roughly, that if there are two initially identical economies and one of them succeeds in consuming less of its output than the other, then after some lapse of time the return on investment will be lower and real wages higher in the high-saving economy than in the low-saving economy. If we think about planned economies we can avoid all difficulties connected with the fact that an attempt to save more may result, in a market economy, in a reduction in saving actually accomplished.

36

My intention in this lecture is to show how the approach to capital theory I adopted this morning stands up when technical progress is taking place. Perhaps the first thing to be done is to call your attention to the peculiar sense in which modern macroeconomists use the phrase 'technical progress'. In every-day speech, talk of technological change calls to mind primarily single discontinuous inventions, like the electric light or the automobile or the electronic computer. Sometimes technological progress occurs in the form of the invention of wholly new products—e.g. television sets—and sometimes in the form of new techniques for producing basically unchanged end-products—e.g. the mechanization of banking or the introduction of artificial fabrics into the making of clothing. But most of this flavor disappears in statistical aggregates.

Economists, who give the impression of having invented the idea of technical progress in the past 6 or 7 years, have something much more pedestrian in mind, and it is perhaps only right that what they have in mind should be described by the pedestrian label of 'increase in output per unit of input'. It is a statistical artifact which arises in the following way. We wish to account for the long-term growth of productive capacity in an economy, perhaps the American, perhaps the Dutch. To do so we have a more or less complete list of determinants or inputs. If the list is truly complete, in the sense that capacity is actually a function of these inputs, then as a matter of algebra the rate of growth of productive capacity is a weighted sum of the rates of growth of the inputs, and the weights are the elasticities of capacity output with respect to each of the inputs or determinants. If there are constant returns to scale, in the sense that doubling or halving all of the inputs (including quality factors like education) will double or halve the social output, then the elasticities will add up to one and the weighted sum becomes a weighted average.

Now it is a fact that when economists have tried to account for the growth of national product in this way there has always been left a substantial residual not easily explained. The rate of growth of output usually exceeds what one can reasonably attribute to the specific list of inputs at hand. And that difference is what we call the rate of increase of output per unit of input or, more picturesquely, the rate of technical progress. Now it is obvious that the more complete the list of inputs, the smaller will be the residual. To take one example, the first investigation of this kind made for the United States worked with a list of inputs limited to capital and labor. Capital was measured by one of the conventional time series purporting to give the real reproduction cost of the stock of durable assets, and labor by the aggregate supply of man-hours. Douglas's early investigations seemed to show that these two inputs could 'account for' all growth just after the turn of the century. But for more recent periods it was found that these two broad inputs together could account for a growth of national product of about 1 per cent a year. Since the national product had a long-term growth rate of about 3 per cent a year, this left 2 per cent a year as the residual increase in output per unit of input. More recently E. F. Denison has made a much more detailed analysis. In particular he extends the list of inputs to include three determinants of the *quality* of labor input: formal education, the more effective utilization of women in the labor force, and the intrinsic effect of shorter working hours on the productivity of labor. One can quarrel with the particular statistical approximations Denison makes. But the general result is only to be expected: labor input corrected for these quality factors has risen much more rapidly than the conventional input of manhours. These new determinants are able to account for more than 1 per cent a year of growth in national product, and thus the residual increase in output per unit of input is reduced from 2 per cent a year to less than 1 per cent a year.

Maybe, with enough effort, the residual can be decreased to zero. Of course that would not mean that technological progress has no long-run importance, but merely that its effects could be imputed back to resources used in research activity and hours worked by scientists and engineers. I doubt this as a practical matter. But in any case even the complete disappearance of the residual would not eliminate the problem I propose to discuss in this lecture: what difference does it make to calculations of the social payoff to investment when we recognize that technology does change? Almost always, technology is assumed to change autonomously; in purest principle there is a deliberate allocation of resources to the generation of technological change—one can think of this as a kind of super-technology. And in the super-technology, investment in tangible capital and investment in generating technical change would presumably be pushed to the point where an extra bit of resources would earn the same rate of return in both uses, after due allowance for risk. But in either case the social return to saving will be affected.

There are at least three basic aspects of the problem to be investigated. The first is to inquire about alternative ways of building technical change into a model of capitalistic production. The conclusions one comes to here affect not only the theoretical side of things but also the empirical procedures by which one tries to isolate in statistical data the influence of changing technology.

The second question that then arises is how to define and calculate the rate of return on investment within such a model. It is not quite so straight-forward a task as in the case without technical progress, because now it is less clear what one ought to be holding constant. When technical change is not occurring, to hold input constant is to hold output constant. That is why the stationary state is such a convenient, if unrealistic, standard of comparison. But when output per unit of all input is increasing, then one is involved in questions of growth; output may rise with unchanging inputs; the natural standard of comparison need not be stationary, in fact can not be stationary in all respects.

The third question to be raised in this context is whether there is a tendency for the private and social rates of return on investment to diverge. Of course, there is no necessary connection between this possibility of externality and the fact of technical progress. There is an abundant literature on external economies and diseconomies, indirect taxes, and inappropriabilities, which create a gap between the social costs or benefits of some economic act and the capturable private costs or benefits to the doer of the act. This analysis can be carried over to acts of investment with very little change. But when technical progress is going on, there are new and different ways in which social and private returns can diverge and it is important for policy reasons to be able to distinguish situations in which there is a presumption that the private economy will over- or under-invest from situations in which there is no such presumption.

On the Classification of Technical Change

Much of the theoretical discussion of technical change has to do with the classification of shifts in technological relationships as labor-saving or capital-saving or neutral. I shall have something to say about that later on, but first I want to remind you of another distinction to be found in the literature, and in life.

When we think about technical progress in the economist's abstract way it is only too natural to imagine a standard production diagram with inputs measured along the axes and a family of equal-output curves of the conventional shape, and to say that when technical progress occurs, the family of equal-output curves shifts in such a way that more output can be produced from given inputs or the same output can be produced with fewer inputs. It is as if the workers in a cheese factory wake up one morning, walk into the same factory they had left the afternoon before, and find that they now know a clever way to produce more cheese. This may not be so implausible as it sounds. The Swedish economist Erik Lundberg has reported that the Horndal iron works in Sweden was left untouched by new investment for some 15 years, yet productivity (output per man-hour) rose on the average by about 2 per cent per year. There remains some question about the sources of that increase in output. It may, as Arrow suggests, represent a kind of learning by experience, with each unit of output contributing something to the production of future output. Or it may reflect simply the passage of time and the improvement of habits and techniques of work, or minor reorganizations within the plant. Or it may reflect primarily changes in the quality of the man-hour worked, through education or changes in standard hours.

Nevertheless it is fair to say that this kind of increase in output per unit of unchanged input does not correspond very well with what actually goes on in the world under the name of technological progress. More often, a technical improvement requires that the concrete inputs, especially the capital inputs, change their form, and sometimes the same is true of the output. A change in the technology of cheese production is much more likely to involve the construction of new factories, with new types of equipment. It may not be easy to say whether there is more equipment or less; for many purposes a reproduction-cost measure will do. I have called this kind of technical change 'embodied' and the other kind, which is purely organizational, may be called 'disembodied'.

I have granted that with embodied technical change it may not be easy to say whether output per unit of 'capital' has increased or decreased, or whether the new method of production is more or less capital-intensive than its predecessor. But since the whole point of the first lecture was to free capital theory from dependence on such statements, I don't think that admission is damaging. But it is not at all a metaphysical question whether technical progress is predominantly embodied or disembodied, whether gross investment is or is not the major vehicle by which new knowledge makes its way into the process of production. If it is not, then a stationary economy, or even one whose conventionally measured gross investment is zero, will find its productivity increasing as rapidly as a growing economy which allocates a substantial fraction of its capacity to conventionally-measured net investment *. If it is, then acts of investment serve the double purpose of adding to the stock of capital goods available for future production and making that stock a little more modern, or raising the average level of technology available for use.

Despite what seems to me to be the overwhelming testimony of casual observation in favor of the embodied-progress model, it appears that the macroeconomic facts can be explained just about equally well with either kind. And since statistical implementation of the disembodied model is somewhat easier, one is tempted to use it. Yet the two models have distinctly different implications about, for example, the short-run consequences of a burst of investment. The trouble is that history does not present us with enough such experiments to provide strong evidence as to which model fits the facts better. Yet this is a question to which every technocrat, and even every detached, observer, would like to know the answer.

---

* The qualification 'conventionally-measured' is necessary here, Paul Samuelson points out, because if 'income' is properly defined as the highest level of consumption attainable without reducing future consumption potential, then an economy whose consumption-potential is rising can not be consuming all its income.

The Rate of Return with Disembodied Technical Progress

The case of disembodied technical progress is straightforward. I turn first to the completely aggregated model I dealt with in the first lecture. The recent surge of interest in output-per-unit-of-input calculations rests explicitly or implicitly on this notion of an aggregate production function shifting through time. This model was analyzed, of course, by Tinbergen as long ago as 1941 and has since been exploited here by Verdoorn and Professor Klaassen; and in the United States and European countries by many authors.

Total gross output depends, at any given level of technology, on the inputs of labor and capital, just as before. But since we are now interested in changes in the level of technology, we must represent it explicitly in our production function. Thus we write $Q = F(K, L; T)$. The parameter T indexes levels of technology. Usually we imagine T changing in time, or even as itself being time. But that is not necessary. We could just as well imagine T as changing as we go from one continent to another. If the production function represented a specific microeconomic technology, such as that for producing cheese, one might expect the technological level T to remain constant for an interval, and then change suddenly when an innovation occurs. But in broad statistical aggregates it is perhaps more natural to think of the overall level of technology as changing gradually and smoothly in time. The disembodied character of technical change in this model is evident from the fact that productive capacity depends on the amount of capital accumulated but not on its age.

44

To calculate a one-period rate of return we perform the standard exercise. Saving a marginal amount of output h at o time 0 enlarges the stock of capital at time 1 to $K_1 + h$, and output to $Q_1 + hF_1 (K_1, L_1; T_1)$. The additional consumption possible is the incremental output itself, plus the surviving part of the originally-saved capital. The rate of return is thus $[hF_1 (K_1, L_1, T_1) + h (1-d)]/h-1 = F_1 (K_1, L_1; T_1) - d$. Just as before the one-period rate of return r_1 is the net marginal product of capital, *at the level of technology ruling in period 1*. A quite similar calculation shows that the two-period rate of return is the solution of $(1 + r_2)^2 = (1 + F_1 (K_1, L_1; T_1) - d) (1 + F_1 (K_2, L_2; T_2) - d)$, and the n-period rate of return satisfies $(1 + r_n)^n = (1 + F_1 (K_1, L_1; T_1) - d) (1 + F_1 (K_2, L_2; T_2) - d) \dots (1 + F_1 CK_n, L_n; T_n) - d)$.

The implications will become a bit more transparent if we make two familiar assumptions: first, that the production function is of the Cobb-Douglas type; and secondly that shifts in the function take place at a constant geometric rate and in a 'neutral' way. Then $F (K_T, L_T; T) = (1 + \lambda)^T K_T^\alpha L_T^{1 - \alpha}$ and for an increment to saving at time 0, we have $r_1 = \alpha (1 + \lambda) (L_1/K_1)^{1 - \alpha} - d$, $(1 + r_2)^2 = (1 + r_1) [1 + \alpha (1 + \lambda)^2 (L_2/K_2)^{1 - \alpha} - d]$, and $(1 + r_n)^n = [1 + \alpha (1 + \lambda) (L_1/K_1)^{1 - \alpha} - d] [1 + \alpha (1 + \lambda)^2 (L_2/K_2)^{1 - \alpha} - d] \dots [1 + \alpha (1 + \lambda)^n (L_n/K_n)^{1 - \alpha} - d]$.

There is something peculiar about this. It looks as if, as time goes on, the one-period rate of return on saving gets indefinitely large, because of the technical progress factor $(1 + \lambda)^t$. Even the n-period rate of return seems to get larger as one takes longer and longer periods. But this is not

45

necessarily true, and the explanation shows how important it is to keep a firm grasp of what is being held constant. It all depends on what happens to L/K during the planned evolution around which we are contemplating variations. Suppose that the fraction of output saved is nearly constant from period to period, and suppose that labor input grows approximately geometrically at rate g. Then it is well-known that in the long-run both output and capital stock will grow at the 'natural' rate $g + \lambda/1 - \alpha$. It is evident, then, that $(L/K)^{1-\alpha}$ will *fall* at a rate close to λ per period and therefore the rate of return on investment will become approximately constant. There is nothing inevitable about this; it just happens that a constant investment quota in this model implies just enough capital-deepening to offset the effect of technical progress on the rate of return. Even so, it is plausible enough—and can be rigorously proved—that the faster the rate of technical progress the higher the rate of return. This is true in the short-run sense that any momentary speed-up in the rate of technical progress means that, for the L and K then ruling, the rate of return on current investment is higher. It is also true in the long-run sense that even after the economy has adapted to the higher rate of technical progress, with the same saving rate, the rate of return on investment will be higher.

Simply to fix approximate orders of magnitude, if α is about $1/4$, and if the capital-gross output ratio is about 2, and the rate of depreciation 5 per cent, then the one-period rate of return is about $7^1/_2$ per cent per year. If the rate of technical change should suddenly go up by 1 percentage point, say from 2 to 3 per cent a year, then in the shortrun the rate of return would rise by almost the full percentage point, to $8^1/_2$ per cent per year.

Of course, in this model one can not simply prescribe a saving rate and a capital-output ratio. Any such combination is possible in the short run, but in time the maintenance of a prescribed saving rate and given rates of increase of labor input and technological level will lead to a particular capital-output ratio, and a particular rate of return on investment. In the model we have been analyzing, the rate of return on new investment will ultimately settle at the value $r = (\alpha/s)$ $[(\lambda/1 - \alpha) + g + d] - d$ where s is the gross saving ratio and n the rate of increase of labor input. Thus with $\alpha = .25$, $s = .10$, $\lambda = .02$, $g = .01$, $d = .05$, we calculate a rate of return equal to about $16^3/_4$ per cent per year. If λ should rise from 2 to 3 per cent per year, the rate of return would rise by more than 3 percentage points to 20 per cent per year.

If these rates of return seem implausibly high one can invent lower ones: if $\alpha = .20$ and $n = .005$ the rates of return are reduced to 11 per cent annually with $\lambda = .02$ and $13^1/_2$ per cent annually if the yearly rate of technical progress should rise to 3 per cent. They would be even lower if we were to calculate with a higher saving rate and lower depreciation rate. I chose my values because it seems more natural to me to exclude houses from the capital stock in such calculations, on the grounds that much of the return from home ownership is non-pecuniary or, in my country at least, a matter of tax advantage.

I should perhaps remind you explicitly that these conclusions about the relation between faster technical progress and a higher rate of return on investment depend on the assumption that the shift in technology is 'neutral' or 'uniform' or at least not capital-saving. With biased technical change the possible consequences are more various, but it would take too long to catalog them.

In the first lecture I spent some time with a model in which saving takes the form of a transfer of labor from a handicraft sector to the production of machines and machine-made consumer goods. That is not a very convenient model to work with, mainly because it does not lend itself at all to empirical analysis, so I shall not treat it in detail. But it is worth a few minutes, because it uncovers some aspects of disembodied technical change which are hidden by the completely aggregated model.

Let me recall the basic structure of the model. In the handicraft industry one worker can produce b units of consumables per year. In the mechanized industry n workers and one machine produce nc units of consumables per year. (Obviously $c > b$, otherwise output per man is greater in the handicraft industry than in the mechanized industry and mechanized production would simply be inefficient). The machine-building sector is also a handicraft and m workers can produce one machine in a year. Since replacement requirements amount to 100 d per cent of the outstanding stock of machines, employment in the machine sector under stationary conditions is mdM and employment in the machine-using sector is nM; thus total employment in the industrial part of the economy is $(md + n) M$. If this were all there were to the economy the possibility of net saving would be uninteresting. If there were more machines relative to available labor than indicated by the required proportionality, it would be impossible both to maintain and operate them. If there were fewer machines, then in effect the surplus labor can be thought of as working in a 'handicraft' industry with $b = 0$. The return to 'saving' would be infinite because no sacrifice of consumption would be necessary; the surplus labor could build and then operate machines.

To introduce the possibility of normal saving and investment, we can add the handicraft consumption sector with $b > 0$. Then that part of the labor supply not employed in machine-using or machine-making is employed making consumer goods by hand; the total output of consumer goods is $C = bL_h + cL_c$. Investment then consists in transferring men from the primitive sector to machine-making and machine-using. The immediate social cost is the loss of the consumption they would have produced in the handicraft sector. The gain is the later flow of output from the enlarged industrial sector.

In this economy the rate of return to saving is (n/m) $[(c/b) - 1] - d$. Technical change can take the form of a change in any of the technological parameters describing the economy. Evidently the rate of return depends only on the ratios n/m and c/b. If n and m both double, c remaining unchanged, it simply means that twice as many men build twice as big a factory requiring twice as many operatives and producing twice as much output; in other words nothing has changed but the size of what we choose to call a machine or factory. If c and b both double then there is a genuine increase in productivity. With the available labor force allocated as before, the output of consumables has doubled. But there is no change in the rate of return because *both* the

49

sacrifice of consumption involved in transferring one man from handicraft production to machine-building and the reward for doing so have doubled.

The kind of technical change that corresponds most closely to a 'neutral' shift in the aggregate production function is a simple increase in c, the output of consumer goods per man in the mechanized industry. Then the allocation of labor among sectors is unaffected. If the change occurs at time 0, then consumption, which had been going along at $bL_h + cL_c$, rises suddenly to $bL_h + c'L_c$. We can repeat this morning's analysis of the consequences of transferring one man to machine-building for one period and then reshuffling so that from period 2 on all proceeds as before but in period 1 the fruits of period 0's saving are consumed. The immediate loss in consumption is b. The stock of machines rises by $1/m$ in period 1, but production of machines in that period can fall to $(1 - d)/m$ below the stationary level. Extra consumption in period 1 is nc'/m from operating the extra machines; in addition, the net addition of labor to the handicraft sector is $(1 - d) - n/m$, whose productive capacity is $b\ [(1 - d) - n/m]$. The rate of return is thus $(n/m)\ [(c'/b) - 1] - d$. In the obvious way, one can build up longer-period rates of return with continuing technical improvement.

But suppose technical change simply increases n to n'. This is actually an unambiguous technical improvement because it means that m men in the machine sector can now equip a larger number of men in the mechanized consumption sector with no change in output *per man*. Remember that with disembodied technical change, even already existing machines undergo this change. Adaptation to this kind of technical progress is not so simple; it is not even straight-forward to say what mode of adaptation from one stationary state to another involves no 'saving'. Imagine an economy that has accumulated and is maintaining a stock of M machines, and therefore has $L_c + L_M = (n + md) M$ men em-ployed in its industrial sector. At the end of the zero'th period, the technocrats learn that in period 1 it will take n' men to operate one machine and produce $n'c$ units of consumer goods. The two simplest modes of adaptation are (a) to keep the stock of machines constant and (b) to keep employment in the mechanized consumption industry con-stant. The latter policy does not achieve a stationary state immediately, and so I concentrate on the first alternative. It is achieved by transferring enough workers from the handicraft industry to man the full stock of M machines, that is $(n' - n) M$ men. The men in the machinery industry must remain to replace the stock of machines. Total output of consumer goods in period 1 will be $n'cM$ in the mechanized industry and $b [L_h (n'-n) M]$ in the handicraft industry. The increment is $(n' - n) (c - b) M$ units of consumer goods.

Now suppose that during the zero'th period the techno-crats had transferred one worker from handicraft production of consumer goods to machine-building. In period 1 the stock of machines would have been higher by $1/m$, requiring an additional n'/m operatives over and above what is needed to man old machines. I need not repeat the calculations; it will be found that the extra saving earns a rate of return of $(n'/m) [(c/b) - 1] - d$ per period. One can easily work out the consequences of a decrease in m or in d, an increase in productivity in machine building or in the durability of machines. There is the same ambiguity about the 'natural' response: whether after a decrease in m, society should hold M constant, and thus transfer workers from machine-building to handicraft, or hold L_M constant and thus (though not instantaneously) increase the stock of machines and draw workers from handicrafts to man them. The latter alternative leads ultimately to a stationary state with higher consumption, but only after a period of lower consumption than the first alternative yields. Fortunately none of this affects the calculation of the rate of return, which is another example of the facility with which this concept avoids 'measurement' problems.

This model provides an easy illustration of the kind of technical progress that might lower the private and social return to saving. The clearest case is an increase in b, the productivity of labor in the hand production of consumer goods. Then an act of investment provides the same maintainable gross flow of consumption to the economy, but the cost in output lost from the handicraft sector is higher and so the net return less. What looks like another possible case, a shift in which both n and m increase, but n/m decreases, turns out to involve some complexity which can not be analyzed clearly without a little more theory than we have established so far.

A Digression

I have said nothing about the labor-saving or machine-saving or even 'capital'-saving character of technical change, for the sufficient reason that to do so would take too much time and would bear very little on the specific subjects under discussion. There is, however, one relevant comment which must be made briefly before one can give a correct account of the possibility that technical progress might lower the rate of return.

My colleague Paul Samuelson has shown that many quite complicated models in which labor is the only non-produced factor of production can be reduced to consideration of the permissible relations between the real wage and the rate of interest. He has called the curve relating these two basic prices the Factor-Price Frontier. When the technology of the model changes, the Factor-Price Frontier shifts. One useful way of characterizing the nature of the shift in technology is through the direction of the shift in the Factor-Price Frontier.

It is instructive to compare the two models I have been analyzing from this point of view. In the aggregated Cobb-Douglas model with a strictly proportional shift factor, $Q = AK^\alpha L^{1-\alpha}$. The rate of return (which we can identify with the rate of interest—notice how I have slipped from purely technocratic notions to market ones—is $\alpha A (L/K)^{1-\alpha} - d = r$. The real wage, which I identify with the marginal product of labor is $(1-\alpha) A/(L/K)^{1-\alpha} = w$. By eliminating L/K we find $w = (1-\alpha) \alpha^{\frac{\alpha}{1-\alpha}} A^{\frac{1}{1-\alpha}} (r+d)^{-\frac{\alpha}{1-\alpha}}$. It is easier to draw the Factor-Price Frontier in the form of a relation between the real wage w and the gross rate of return $r + d$. If the level of technology should rise by 1 per cent (A become 1.01 A), the Factor-Price Frontier shifts outward and the shift (in this special case) can be described in several ways. One can say that for each value of $r + d$, w

rises in the same proportion, namely by a factor $(1.01)^{\frac{1}{1-\alpha}}$. Alternatively one can say that for each value of w, $r + d$ shifts to the right by the factor $(1.01)\frac{1}{\alpha}$. Or third, we can say that it is possible for *both* $r + d$ *and* w to increase by a factor 1.01. The Factor-Price Frontier shifts upward in a constant proportion; it shifts rightward in a constant propertion; and it shifts outward along rays in a constant proportion. Only for the Cobb-Douglas function do all these descriptions come to the same thing.

Now think of our other model for a moment. The constant b, the productivity of labor in the handicraft sector, plays the role of a real wage in that model, so that its Factor-Price Frontier can be written $(r + d) = (n/m) [(c/w) - 1]$. The general shape is not very different from that for the aggregate Cobb-Douglas. But a little experimentation shows that changes in the parameters n, m, c, and d lead to somewhat different kinds of shifts in the Factor-Price Frontier. A 1 per cent increase in c does have the property that at every gross profit rate $r + d$ the real wage increases by a factor 1.01, so the curve has a proportionate upward shift. But the other two descriptions do not apply. To have a proportionate rightward shift there must be an increase in n or a decrease in m. And to permit a proportionate increase in both $(r + d)$ and w, one must have an equiproportionate increase in c and in n/m.

It seems to me to be a matter of little or no importance which of these shift patterns one chooses to call 'neutral'. The movement of the whole Factor-Price Frontier contains most of the information one wants for analyzing the consequences of shifts in technology.

In a competitive market economy, it is clear that the phenomenon we call technical progress can only shift the Factor-Price Frontier outward (or upward or rightward). If the 'old' technology is not somehow forgotten, then the 'old' Factor-Price Frontier and the 'new' one can never cross. For if they could, then it would have to be the case that for some real wage, the rate of interest is lower under the new technology than under the old. But then if that real wage were ever to rule in the market, capitalists would chosse to use the old, unforgotten, technology and earn the higher rate of return corresponding to it. In other words, if the factor-price frontiers for two alternative states of technology should actually cross, then the new technology can not be economic at all factor prices, and will not be adopted if the particular factor price configuration ruling does not make it profitable to do so. Thus the operative Factor-Price Frontier for the two co-existing technologies is the outer envelope of their separate Factor-Price Frontiers.

In the two-sector fixed-coefficient model we have been analyzing, the productivity of labor in the handicraft consumption industry plays the role of a real wage. It is the social cost of labor to the industrial sector. Thus it is possible for an increase in b to lower the rate of return on capital; the Factor-Price Frontier shifts outward, but the 'real wage' rises enough to drive the rate of return below its previous level. As long as b remains constant, no improvement in technical knowledge can lower the rate of return on investment. If the technocrats have access both to the old set of coefficients and the new ones, they will find it inefficient to adopt a new technology which involves a lower rate of return. This is not because they 'collect' the rate of return like ordinary capitalists, but simply because a bigger gain in output would be achievable for any given sacrifice of current consumption using the old technology. A slightly different analysis is necessary to determine whether it would be better to operate already existing machines under the old or the new technology, but the very thought itself suggests that the assumption of disembodied technical change has been stretched as far as it will go.

The Rate of Return under Embodied Technical Progress

I must now discuss what seems to me to be the more realistic situation, in which each level of technology requires its own characteristic types of capital equipment. There is no need for me to elaborate on the structure of this kind of model; I have discussed it in several papers and so have Johansen, Koyck and Mrs. 't Hooft, Klaassen, Phelps, Massell, and no doubt others. There is a choice whether to assume that possibilities of immediate substitution exist between labor and specific concrete capital goods belonging to a particular level of technology, or to suppose that even within a particular level of technology, fixed proportions rule in the shortrun, or *ex post* while any change in the degree of capital intensity of production requires the construction of appropriate types of capital equipment. The latter assumption seems more suitable for short-run analysis or for dealing with narrowly-defined production processes. For studying the long-run and gross aggregates, it may be closer to the truth to permit direct subsitution between labor and capital because something very like this happens in a growing economy through the slow replacement of one kind of capital good by another and one type of final output by another. The direct substitution model has the additional advantage of being tractable enough for pencil-and-paper calculations. The model with fixed proportions *ex post* and variable proportions *ex ante* has the difficult property that its current and future behavior may depend on the precise sequential story of its recent past (*i.e.* on the existing mixture of old heterogeneous capital goods) rather than on any summary numbers. The only way I have found to deal with it is by experiments with a computing machine. In any case, both models seem to lead to similar results as respects the one question I am pursuing here. So I shall deal with the simpler substitution model, and indeed only with a special case of that.

When technological level is embodied in durable capital assets, the economy is like an archaeological digging, with layers of older capital equipment representing lower levels of technical knowledge. But the archaeological analogy breaks down, because many technological layers may be in active operation at the same time. Old and obsolete factories can produce actively so long as they earn any excess over prime costs. They are obsolete because they cannot earn the going rate of profit on their reproduction cost; and the market will value obsolete capital at less than reproduction cost, indeed at just that value which permits it to earn the going rate of profit. The capital loss which drives the price of old capital below reproduction cost is the market's signal to the investment sector to stop producing plant and equipment of old and outdated type. It is a very important part of what I have to say that such capital losses caused by obsolescence must, in a progressive economy, come to be expected by investors. As I have mentioned, obsolescent plant and equipment need not disappear; it can continue in use so long as it can earn any quasi-rent at all. If the substitutability between variable inputs and capital is sufficiently easy, then old capital will not be driven out of production until it wears out. If there is only limited substitutability, however, eventually rising real wages and other costs will render obsolete capital wholly uneconomic and it will cease to operate.

In the model with disembodied technical progress, the notion of obsolescence simply does not occur. It is ruled out by the assumption that old capital shares equally with new in technical progress. Under that assumption, we have seen that the social rate of return to investment coincides with the marginal product of capital, when the technology is smooth enough to admit marginal products. Ordinary market theory tells us that when capital markets are competitive, the private rate of return to saving will in equilibrium coincide with the marginal product of a dollar's worth of capital and therefore with the social return to saving. Our simple fixed-proportions model shows how, even when there are no marginal products defined, a social rate of return to investment can be defined. And my remarks on the Factor-Price Frontier prove that perfectly functioning markets will equate the private and social rates of return on acts of saving and investment. My next task is to show that in the model with embodied technical progress, the fact of expectable obsolescence reduces the private rate of return on saving *below* the marginal product of capital as one might ordinarily calculate it. But this discrepancy is fully reflected in a parallel difference between the marginal product of capital and the social rate of return on saving. So once again the private and social rates of return coincide.

This is easy to prove only in one special case and I shall limit myself to it. This is the case when technical progress is 'purely capital-augmenting' in the sense that after an improvement has occurred one unit of capital (measured in replacement cost) and x units of labor can produce precisely what $1/(1 + \lambda)$ units of capital and x units of labor could produce before the change. The coverage of this special case is wider than one would think, because if the production function for each given level of technology is Cobb-Douglas, and if technological shifts leave the Cobb-Douglas exponents invariant, then the shifts may always be thought of as purely capital-augmenting. What makes this special case so easy to discuss is the following proposition: if embodied technical change is purely capital augmenting, so $Q_v(t) = F[K_v(t), L_v(t), v] = F[A_v K_v(t), L_v(t)]$ (where the subscript v indicates that the output is produced at time t using the surviving capital goods embodying the level of technology current at time v with the labor assigned to those capital goods, and Av is an increasing sequence showing how the level of technology has risen), then the maximum output producible at time t, say $Q(t)$, can be expressed as a function of the total supply of labor, say $L(t)$, and a single number $J(t)$ which is a productivity-weighted sum of the surviving capital goods representing all earlier technological levels. $J(t)$ may be called an 'effective stock of capital':

$J(t) = \Sigma A_v K_v(t)$. Instead of having to calculate the output produced from each fossil-level of plant and equipment, we can simply say $Q(t) = F[J(t), L(t)]$.

To see the utility of this simplification, one need only remember what is involved in calculating a one-period rate of return. The thought-experiment is to sacrifice one unit of consumption at time t in favor of investment, and then ask what is the largest increment of consumption that can be enjoyed at time $t+1$ without impairing consumption possibilities in any later period. When productive capacity can be expressed in terms of available labor supply and an effective stock of capital, this last condition means that the effective stock of capital bequeathed to period $t+2$ must be no smaller than would have been the case had the extra saving in period t and the extra consumption in period $t+1$ not taken place. (For the calculation to turn out quite this simply, I also need the assumption that capital goods depreciate geometrically, with a fraction d disappearing each year.)

In year 0, the technocrats arrange to save an extra h of generalized output. Since the 'productivity weight' attached to investment in year 0 is 1, the act of saving adds h to effective capital for year 1, and h times the marginal product of effective capital to output in year 1. Since a fraction d of this increment will perish in year 1, $(1-d)h$ will survive as part of effective capital for year 2. Thus society need save less of year 1's output than it otherwise would. But since a unit of saving in year 1 adds $(1+\lambda)$ to effective capital, society can reduce its saving by $(1-d)h/(1+\lambda)$. Thus k, the consumption bonus available in year 1 is the extra output, h times the marginal product of capital in year 1, puls

$h(1-d)/(1+\lambda)$. The rate of return is $(k-h)/h =$ marginal product of capital in year $1-(d+\lambda)/(1+\lambda)$.

More formally, at time 0, one has $Q_0 = F(J_0, L_0) = C_0 + I_0$, where I_0 is gross investment. Similarly at time 1, one has $Q_1 = C_1 + I_1 = F(J_1, L_1) = F[(1-d)J_0 + I_0, L_1]$, where the last equality comes about because the effective stock of capital J, consists of the survivors from time 0, $(1-d)J_0$ where d is the depreciation rate, plus the gross investment of period 0. Finally and similarly J_2, the effective stock of capital left over at time 2 is $J_2 = (1-d)J_1 + (1+\lambda)I_1 = (1-d)^2 J_0 + (1-d)I_0 + (1+\lambda)I_1$, where λ is the rate of *embodied* technical progress, and J_2 is to be held constant while we trade off consumption at time 0 for consumption at time 1. Since J_0 is in any case given by history, this means that all maneuvering must leave $(1-d)I_0 + (1+\lambda)I_1$ constant. But $(1-d)I_0 + (1+\lambda)I_1 = (1-d)(Q_0-C_0) + (1+\lambda)(Q_1-C_1) = (1-d)(Q_0-C_0) + (1+\lambda)[F((1-d)J_0 + Q_0 - C_0, L_1) - C_1]$. From this it is easily calculated that a small sacrifice h of C_0 results in an increment $k = h[F_1, (J_1, L_1) + (1-d)/(1+\lambda)]$ so that the social rate of return on investment is $k/h - 1 = F_1(J_1, L_1) - (d+\lambda)/(1+\lambda)$. The term $F_1(J_1, L_1)$ is the gross marginal product of new investment, and $F_1 - d$ is the net marginal product of new investment. Thus the social rate of return on new investment falls short of the net marginal product by an amount which is to all intents and purposes equal to λ, the rate at which the specific productivity of capital goods is rising.

This is an important result. It says that there is a social equivalent to obsolescence. This in turn means, as we shall see in a moment, that the occurrence of embodied technical progress by itself creates no divergence between the private and social yield on investment. The social equivalent of obsolescence is, of course, not a simple capital loss. It represents, rather, the fact that it is more costly to increase next year's capital stock through this year's saving than it will be to increase the following year's capital stock through next year's saving. As James Tobin and Arthur Okun have put this point: 'Why should we save now when our saving produces nothing better than jet airplanes, while the saving of our children will produce transport rockets to take us, or rather them, to Europe in 10 minutes?' The return to current saving is reduced by the fact that current saving adds less to future consumption-potential than next year's saving would.

I have mentioned that the amount by which the return on investment falls short of the net marginal product of capital is about equal to the rate of improvement in the productivity of capital. That may be a substantial number. We are used to thinking of 'total' productivity as increasing by 1 or 2 per cent annually. The disembodied equivalent would be a Cobb-Douglas production function $(1.02)^t K_t^{1/3} L_t^{2/3}$. If this described the technology, the output producible from any combination of (new or old) capital and labor rises autonomously by 2 per cent a year. The same potential for growth would require a purely capital-augmenting rate of progress of 6 per cent a year; since the elasticity of output with respect to capital is $1/3$, it takes a 6 per cent increase in 'effective capital' to generate a 2 per cent increase in output capacity. Thus a 15 per cent net marginal product of capital is the equivalent of only 9 per cent annual return on investment. Or, to put it differently, the correct marginal product of capital, after allowing for correct economic depreciation is not 15 per cent, but 9 per cent. It is even possible, though hardly likely, that a rapid rate of embodied technical progress in an already highly capitalized economy could make the rate of return on investment negative. In the disembodied case we found that other things equal, the higher the rate of neutral technological progress the higher the rate of return. In the case of embodied technical change it is perfectly possible, and not even terribly unlikely, that a higher rate of neutral technological progress should mean a *lower* rate of return. Indeed, if society today suddenly expects a higher rate of technical progress for the future than it expected yesterday, then society must revise *downward* the rate of return it expects to earn on current saving.

It is commonplace that anticipated obsolescence reduces the return any private entrepreneur can expect to realize on an investment. We have just seen that there is an analogous effect for society. Now we can go one step further. The effects are exactly parallel; if the social and private marginal products of effective capital are identical, then so are the rates of return to new investment. To see this we need only calculate the private rate of return in year 0. The gross rental earned in a competitive market by a unit of up-to-date capital is the gross marginal product $F_1(J_1, L_1)$. To get the net rate of return we must deduct the loss in value on account of physical depreciation and any capital gains or losses that may occur. Suppose there were no physical deterioration. It would nevertheless be true that in year 1 one unit of output will purchase a capital good 100 λ per cent more productive, i.e. one that will earn a rent $1 + \lambda$ times that earned by a one-year old unit of capital. To equalize the return per dollar, the price of a one-year old capital good must fall to $1/(1+\lambda)$. The loss in value is thus $1 - 1/(1+\lambda) = \lambda(1+\lambda)$. In addition, the investor will find himself not with one unit of one-year old capital, but with $1 - d$ units, because there is physical depreciation. He will thus expect and experience a total loss in value of $(d+\lambda)/(1+\lambda)$ of which $d/(1+\lambda)$ is depreciation and $\lambda/(1+\lambda)$ is capital loss because of obsolescence. The net private rate of return is therefore $F_1(J_1, L_1) - (d+\lambda)/(1+\lambda)$, the same as the social rate of return. (The basis for this calculation is implicit in my 1959 paper on embodied technical progress and quite explicit in the 1961 paper of Koyck and Mrs. 't Hooft-Welvaars).

To summarize, when technical change is embodied, and hence obsolescence is a fact of life, the private and social rates of return remain equal, but both are less than the conventionally-calculated marginal product of new capital, perhaps substantially less. And more rapid technical progress, or an acceleration of technical progres, may actually lower both private and social rates of return.

I have no time to repeat this analysis for the fixed coefficient model with separate consumption-good and investment-good sectors. The story is, however, quite similar. If technical change is embodied in each year's crop of machines, and if its qualitative character is 'purely capital-augmenting' (which means in this case an increase in n, the number of men operating a single machine, or a decrease in m the number of men needed to make a machine, with no change in

c or b, the output per man by the two techniques in the consumption goods sector), then one can summarize the productive capacity of the economy in terms of an effective stock of machines. And the rate of return on saving is reduced by an amount reflecting the rate of obsolescence inflicted on old machines by new ones. I hope I have made my point that the version of neo-classical capital theory sketched in these lectures is in no way dependent on the possibility of smooth substitution.

Private and Social Returns from Investment

In discussing the payoff to investment under embodied technical progress I have repeatedly emphasized the equality of the private and the social rates of return. The point seemed worth making both because it is not entirely obvious that there is an exact social analog to the private risk of obsolescence, and because the literature is occasionally unclear about the distribution of the benefits of technical progress. But I hope I have not given the impression that in fact the private and social returns to investment are identical. I have been demonstrating the much weaker proposition that if the private and social marginal products of capital coincide, then the private and social rates of return will coincide. To put it differently, I have been trying to show that the mere fact of embodied technical progress does not itself drive a wedge between the private and social rates of return, if there were no wedge before.

Naturally, when technical progress is embodied in capital goods, differences between the private and social rates of return can arise in all the ways in which they can arise when technical progress is disembodied or when there is no technical progress at all. Monopolistic restrictions and external effects in production and consumption can lead to misallocation of resources in a technically progressive economy as well as in a stationary one.

Recently Kenneth Arrow has produced an interesting new analysis which does indeed illustrate a way that embodied technical progress can create its own special kind of gap between the private and social rates of return to capital investment. It is a difficult model to test empirically, but there can be little doubt that it points to a real fact of life. Arrow assumes, as I have done, that each item of capital equipment represents the highest level of technology known at the time of its construction. But whereas I have been assuming that the level of technological knowledge rises simply with the passage of time, Arrow postulates that technical progress arises out of ecperience and experience consists of gross investment. Thus, in the model I have been analyzing, if gross investment were to stop for a year technological knowledge would continue to accumulate. It would have no effect on the process of production because it is not yet embodied in new capital goods. But the knowledge is there to be used, and if gross investment occurs again in the year following the lapse of time it shows itself in the higher productivity of new capital. The longer the time interval, the higher the productivity at the end. In Arrow's model when there is no gross investment there is no accumulation of knowledge. Let gross investment stop for a year or two years or ten years; whenever it starts up again it will start at the same technological level because nothing will have been learned in the meanwhile.

In some respects this model is like the ones I have already discussed in this lecture. Private investment suffers capital losses because of gradual obsolescence. There is a complication because the rate of obsolescence to be expected depends on the volume and timing of future investment, not simply on the passage of time. (But actually something very like this happens in all models of capital accumulation, especially if there is only limited substitutability between concrete capital goods and other factors of production.) Also as in other models, the social attractiveness of current investment is diminished by the fact that it must compete against the possibility of investment in even more productive capital goods in the future.

But now a wholly new element is added. A planned economy contemplating a marginal increase in current investment will take account of the fact that each such increment constitutes some 'learning'; if current investment were higher, each unit of capital created during the whole future would be more productive. This is because, in the Arrow model, the technological efficiency of newly-produced capital depends on the cumulative volume of gross investment in the past. A decision to increase investment now, other things equal, means that each planned future act of investment will have the advantage of a larger volume of cumulated past capital formation, and will therefore be more productive. This 'learning' aspect adds something to the social rate of return on current investment. But in an ordinary market economy, however perfectly competitive, there is no way for a private investor to capture any part of the added productivity that his investment contributes to all future investment. It is as if all current investment involved *ipso facto* a kind of research, the results of which are automatically in the public domain, and cannot be appropriated and sold.

The result of all this is that the private rate of return on investment falls short of the social rate of return. Entirely apart from monopolistic restrictions, one must expect the rate of investment in a private-enterprise economy to be less than optimal. Most advanced economies have recognized this with respect to research and development activity itself. Public funds finance much industrial research in most such economies. The importance of Arrow's model is to suggest that there may be a case for extending similar treatment to fixed investment for similar reasons.

In the next lecture I will present some estimates of social rates of return to fixed investment, and discuss a few of their implications for public policy and for economic growth. I would not wish to be burned at the stake either for the estimates or for their implications. But I will say about them what the inveterate gambler said about the dishonest roulette wheel: 'I know the wheel is crooked, but it's the only game in town'. Besides, one important function of research is to suggest topics for further research; and that test the next lecture will pass with flying colors.

CHAPTER III

TECHNICAL PROGRESS, THE AGGREGATE PRO-DUCTION FUNCTION AND THE RATE OF RETURN

If there is any truth to what I have been saying, then the rate of return on investment is an important number to know in any real economy. Policy decisions involving the direction of investment or the determination of the overall volume of investment should properly rest on estimates of the rates of return for individual projects or for the economy as a whole. Economists have too often been content with poor substitutes like capital-output ratios. I suppose, or at least I hope, this is because average quantities are always easier to measure than the more appropriate marginal quantities. I mean marginal in the strict other-things-equal sense, not in the loose sense of comparing increments over time. If such is indeed the case, then applied capital theory is a field in which more research urgently needs to be done.

Even in a market economy, at least in one enjoying approx-imately full employment, some knowledge of the rate of return would be useful not only in the formulation of fiscal and monetary policy for the long run, but also in estimating the prospects for private investment demand. Information about the rate of return can easily be converted into an estimate of the effect on economic growth of whatever private and public investment is undertaken. The qualification about near-full employment is important. The rate of return, as it is used in these lectures, is primarily a technological concept unaffected by the possibilities of deficient effective demand. It seems likely that subjective rates of return on real investment were zero or negative in the U.S. during the depression of the 1930's. But this was a consequence of hardened expectations of poor markets. In my technocratic sense the real social rate of return at full employment could not have been very different in 1933 from what it had been five years earlier.

It is cold comfort to be told that the rate of return is an important number for economic analysis without being told a way to find it out. How then should economists go about estimating the social rate of return? I do not pretend to know the right answer to this question. Perhaps all that one can say is that the more methods we try, the more answers we will get; and out of the comparison may come both an idea as to which method is best and an indication of how uncertain the results are.

Estimating the Rate of Return

One possibility that presents itself is to rely on private rates of profit as rough indicators of social rates of return in different lines of industry. As a first approximation there is something to be said for this idea, but there are also several things to be said against it. First, private profits may contain an element of monopoly profit which ought not to be reflected in estimates of the social returns to investment. Secondly, there are still other reasons why the market prices of certain goods and services may not reflect their true utility to society; that is why the literature of economic planning is so concerned with the distinction between market prices and accounting prices. Third, private profits contain an allowance for risk. But risk is a quantity which can be reduced by pooling; that is the principle of insurance. For this reason social risk tends to be less than private risk, and the social return to investment higher than the private return, when both are corrected for the relevant risks. This discrepancy is smaller the more extensive the possibility of insurance or of diversification, or the more extensive the loss-offset provision in the tax law. But no private insurance scheme or diversified enterprise approaches in coverage the pooling of risk that is possible to society as a whole, so some discrepancy may remain. Fourth, there are the classical technological external economies and diseconomies, the smoke nuisances and water pollution, the unpaid-for third-party benefits, which drive wedges here and there between the private and social profitability of particular investments. Fifth, there are difficulties connected with business and personal taxation. To know whether before-tax or after-tax profit rates are relevant one must know something about the incidence of business taxation, and that may be a harder problem than the one we started with.

One could think of still other reasons why a simple inference from private profit to social benefit would not be legitimate. For large investment projects in small countries, and even for small public investment in large countries, the best approach is probably direct calculation of the expected cost and benefit streams. As an impractical economic theorist, I am after bigger game—or at least more exciting sport—and I propose to estimate the social rate of return by first estimating an aggregate production function. I could easily think of five reasons why this approach won't work perfectly. Just for example, aggregate output is necessarily measured by some market price or factor cost total from the national accounts. But then some of the same difficulties that bedevil the interpreter of private rates of profit will be obstacles to the use of an aggregate production function. In addition, there are all the usual problems about dealing with index numbers or gross aggregates as if they were well-defined physical quantities. These problems are amply discussed in the literature, but you are too polite and I too self-indulgent to bring them up now.

I had hoped at one time to be able to produce for this occasion a comparison of production functions and rates of return in the United States and in the Netherlands. But I could not find, in the published Dutch statistical material available to me, long enough time series to permit a production function analysis. It is obvious, after all, that the most one can hope to capture in an aggregate production function is an interpretation of trend movements in input and output. Year-to-year changes are subject to too many other influences, like shifts in the industrial composition of output, or in the aggregate pressure of demand. Even a generous interpretation of 'long-run' suggests that one ought to have data extending over several decades.

Quite recently, the IFO-Institute in Munich has published the necessary raw materials for a production function analysis of Germany. The data are time series for deflated national product, man-hours worked, deflated gross and net fixed investment and capital stock covering the period 1925—1938, 1950—1957. * Dr. Gehrig and Dr. Kuhlo published at the

* *IFO-Studien*, 7.Jg, 1961, Heft 1/2, various articles.

same time their own production function for Germany. Their methods differ from mine in several respects, none of which seems very important. But one important difference is that they allow for technical progress only in its completely disembodied form, whereas I am especially interested in the effects of embodied technical change. Most desirable of all would be a statistical treatment which could separate and measure the effects of both kinds of technical change. There is no formal obstacle in the way of such an analysis, but I have serious doubts whether a few highly autocorrelated and intercorrelated time series contain so much subtle information. Since the pure disembodied and pure embodied models are each capable of explaining the basic facts separately, there can hardly be much gain in putting them together. I know of no really successful attempt to treat both kinds of technical change simultaneously, and my own attempts have come out badly. Here is another research problem awaiting a clever idea.

There should be some general interest in a comparison of production functions in Germany and the United States. During the 1950's, the West German economy invested heavily and grew rapidly. During most of the same decade, the American economy had a low rate of investment and a fairly low rate of growth, even at full employment. That there is a relation between the investment quota and the rate of growth of potential output no one can doubt. It is in part the same relation we have been studying under the name of the rate of return. But this perception is sometimes carried to the point of suggesting that if the United States were to invest the same fraction of its national product as Germany it could grow as fast. That can hardly be true, because there are other factors of production besides capital, because the law of diminishing returns suggests that the payoff to investment may be smaller in a country with as much accumulated capital as the United States, and because if technological progress is embodied in new capital the responsiveness of output to investment depends on the size and age of the existing stock of capital. I hope that some direct light can be thrown on these questions by a comparison of production functions for the two countries.

One can think of still other important questions of analysis and policy whose resolution would be much easier if we knew something about relative rates of return in different countries. For example, if for one reason or another the true rate of return to investment is lower in the United States than elsewhere, then it would be natural, as many economists suspect, for the U.S. to be a long-run exporter of capital to the rest of the world, and the current state of affairs may be an enduring one in that respect. Furthermore, if relative saturation with capital has driven the private rate of return in the U.S. below the rate elsewhere, and if—as I believe—monetary policy does have domestic effects, then the United States *needs* lower interest rates than other countries. And the prescription commonly offered, not least by the Dutch, I am told, that the United States balance of payments deficit be repaired by a determined resort to high interest rates may be a much more complicated proposition than it sounds.

It is time to turn to the facts. It may well be too flattering to describe what I am about to relate to you as 'facts' but, whatever they are, it is time to turn to them.

An Aggregate Production Function Model

The basic model I have used for both Germany and the United States is one discussed in earlier lectures. Plant and equipment embodies the latest or 'best-practice' technology at the time it is produced. It does not share at all in later technical progress, but all the original possibilities of direct substitution between labor and capital goods are retained throughout the lifetime of the capital goods. The production function for a given level of technology, embodied in a given 'vintage' of capital goods, is of the Cobb-Douglas type, but the elasticities or Cobb-Douglas exponents are the same for all vintages. Newer capital is distinguished from older capital by being more productive, but not by a different elasticity.

Each year, the available supply of labor is distributed over the existing stock of capital goods of different vintages in an efficient way, so that the aggregate output produced by the economy in factories of all ages is a maximum. This entails that older, less efficient, capital is operated less labor-intensively than newer, because all workers must earn the same wage regardless of the age of the factory they enter every morning. As I mentioned last time, this model has the nice property that aggregate productive capacity can be represented by a Cobb-Douglas function in total labor supply and an 'effective stock of capital'. This effective stock of capital is a weighted sum of the surviving stocks of capital of all vintages, with the weights reflecting the higher intrinsic productivity of newer capital goods.

Formally, the aggregate production function can be written $Q_t = AJ_t^\alpha L_t^{1-\alpha}$ where Q_t is potential or capacity output, L_t is the full employment supply of labor, and $J_t = \Sigma (1+\lambda)^v K_v(t)$, with λ representing the geometric rate of technical progress and $Kv(t)$ the quantity of capital goods constructed in year v (and thus enjoying the level of technology $(1+\lambda)^v$) and surviving in year t.

To estimate a production function of this type requires data on potential output, the supply of labor, and the equivalent stock of capital. For the United States I have used a specially-constructed series for real output which I have called Business Output, in 1954 prices. It represents that part of domestic gross product which is produced with privately-owned plant and equipment. It is in fact the Gross National Product after deduction of product originating in government, in households and certain non-profit institutions, in the rest of the world, and in the services of houses. This last deduction is necessary because I have excluded houses from the stock of capital. For Germany the output series is the Gross National Product itself, also in 1954 prices, and houses and government-owned capital are included in the stock of capital. This is one of a number of important discrepancies in the data for the two countries, and we will have to allow for it in interpreting the results. The measurement of output presents another problem. In principle we need a measure of potential output while the data give us only actual output in each year, influenced by varying levels of effective demand. To overcome this difficulty I have included the unemployment rate as a variable in the production function, and the numerical results indicate that it copes fairly successfully with the changes in actual output brought about by cyclical fluctuations.

Since business-cycle changes in labor input are absorbed by the unemployment-rate variable, the appropriate measure of labor in the production function is not employment but the full-employment supply of labor. Both for the United States and Germany there are available annual estimates of the number of man-hours that would have been worked under full-employment conditions. These make allowance for the long-run changes in standard hours per week or per year. I must recognize that they do not allow for the slow increase in the quality of the representative man-hour as the education, skill, and health of the labor force improve from decade to decade. This omission will have the effect that some of the increase in output attributable to education, training, and medical science will appear as 'technological progress'. There may also be some distortion of the shape of the production function, which can only be remedied by better measurement of labor input. Research now under way both in the Netherlands and in the United States may soon make this remedy available, but for the moment I have done nothing about it.

The hardest part of the statistical job is the construction of a time series for the effective stock of capital. I have 'solved' this problem by brute force. To begin with, we have no usable outside information about the pace of technological progress. So I assume, with everyone else, that it can be approximated by a constant annual rate of improvement. For any particular annual rate of progress, say 2 per cent a year, I have built up time series of the effective stock of capital from the past record of gross investment and whatever information about the length of life of equipment and buildings is available. As you know, information on the durability of capital is fragmentary, and what there is is often implausible. But such assumptions have to be made, even by statisticians who are simply trying to measure the conventional stock of capital, and I have used whatever they use. In the German data, for example, the assumption is that machinery lasts for about 26 years and buildings almost forever (presumably because of repairs and maintenance expenditures which are unfortunately not included in the gross investment figures). In any case—this is no business for a man with a sensitive stomach—given any concrete assumption about durability, a long enough real gross investment series, and an arbitrary rule of technical progress, one can compute the effective stock of capital step by step according to the definition, weighting each year's gross investment with the appropriate productivity factor and dropping out old capital according to the assumed life table. I have done this both for Germany and the United States for rates of technical progress equal to .00 (which yields the conventional stock of capital), .02, .03, .04, and .05. The empirical raw materials for the production function are thus complete.

Results for the United States

In describing the numerical results I shall allow implicitly for the influence of the unemployment rate in accounting for variations in effective demand. This gives sensible results for the U.S. and makes little difference for Germany, because the whole postwar decade is regarded as one of full employment anyway. Thus I speak only of the implied relation between potential output on the one hand and inputs of man-hours and 'effective capital' on the other. In principle, the correct estimation procedure is to try successive rates of embodied technical progress until one finds the one that gives the best fit. In practice, it turns out that rates of progress between 2 and 5 per cent a year give almost uniformly good fits in both countries. I take no credit for this; the underlying time series all have strong trends and it would take a remarkably bad model to give a poor fit. I can not honestly claim to have made a very accurate estimate of the rate at which the productivity of new investment improves in these countries, and so I shall try to restrict myself to drawing only those inferences which don't depend very much on that kind of precision.

In dealing with the United States I have simply assumed the existence of constant returns to scale. For Germany I have made estimates both with this assumption and without it. As usually happens, when the assumption of constant returns to scale is not made, the data tend to yield a presumption of sharply increasing returns to scale. Fortunately, the main points I want to make about the rate of return on investment are not much affected. The answers to many other important questions about economic growth are affected by the nature of returns to scale, so this is a matter deserving further research.

For the United States I list in Table 1 the estimates of the elasticities of capacity output with respect to labor and effective capital for rates of technical progress $\lambda = .00$, $.02$, $.03$, $.04$, and $.05$.

Table 1

λ Rate of increase of productivity of capital	α Elasticity of output with respect to capital		1 — α Elasticity of output with respect to labor	R^2
.00	1.2377	(.0993)	— 0.2377	.9622
.02	0.6323	(.0364)	0.3677	.9789
.03	0.5054	(.0270)	0.4946	.9816
.04	0.4160	(.0214)	0.5940	.9828
.05	0.3611	(.0176)	0.6389	.9845

These figures verify the earlier remark that the goodness of fit can not be relied upon to pick out the 'right' rate of technical progress. Even the combined assumption that there is constant returns to scale and no technical progress gives a very high correlation, though it also gives the nonsense result that the marginal contribution of labor is negative. It is true that the correlation gets better for higher rates of technical change. But the improvement is slight and, given the character of the underlying statistical material, I would not be inclined to place much emphasis on it.

It may strike you that 4 or 5 per cent a year is a high rate of technical progress for an economy whose output has grown only at 3 per cent a year on the average over the long period, and whose labor force and stock of capital have been growing too. The apparent paradox is resolved by the recollection that λ is the annual rate at which the productivity of new capital improves. But a 1 per cent increase in the effective stock of capital yields only an α per cent increase in output, if α is the elasticity of output with respect to effective capital. So a rough estimate of the contribution of technical progress to the growth of output can be obtained by multiplying each λ and its corresponding α. That explains why a higher rate of technical change is associated with a lower estimate of the elasticity of output with respect to effective capital: the statistical procedure is trying to explain the observed rate of growth of output. When I take λ as 2 per cent, 3 per cent, 4 per cent, and 5 per cent the estimated contribution of technical change to the rate of growth of output goes only from 1.3 per cent to 1.5 per cent to 1.7 per cent to 1.8 per cent per year.

The traditional reason for accepting the higher rates of technical progress is the identification of the Cobb-Douglas elasticity with the share of income from capital in total income. If the American economy does behave in such a way as to mimic a competitive market, then the right order of magnitude for the elasticity of output with respect to capital is somewhere between .30 and .40. Since output is gross output, an allowance for depreciation has to be included in income from property. I use data for the corporate sector of the American economy as a good approximation to the whole business sector. In reasonably prosperous years since 1929, the compensation of employees has amounted to just about 64 per cent of the corporate gross product. That makes the elasticity of 0.36 with λ = .05 look very good. From some points of view, however, gross product is not the appropriate measure of output. The market price of corporate output contains a variable amount of indirect taxation and it is not clear how one ought to allow for it, or whether a factor cost measure of output would not be better. Since 1929, compensation of employees has averaged about 70 per cent of corporate gross product net of indirect taxes. Probably I should simply conclude that an α between 0.30 and 0.36, and therefore a rate of increase in the productivity of new investment between 5 and 6 per cent a year, would be most appropriate. I regret not having performed a set of calculations for $\lambda = .06$; perhaps that oversight can be remedied later.

Perhaps the simplest rough summary of these estimates is to say that between 1929 and 1957, real potential Business Output grew at an average annual rate of about 3 per cent. If we adopt the production function with the productivity of new capital growing at 5 per cent per year and $\alpha = .36$, then technical progress accounts on the average for a growth in output of 1.8 per cent a year. The full-employment supply of man-hours grew at about one-half of one per cent a year and contributed three-tenths of one per cent to the growth rate. During the same period the conventional stock of plant and equipment grew at a rate of about 2.1 per cent a year and accounted for eight-tenths of one per cent in the growth rate. This story has been told often and what I have to add to it concerns the rate of return on capital. I will return to that central subject after having described the numerical results for Germany.

Results for Germany

In interpreting the results for Germany, it is important to remember that the definitions of output and capital are different in some respects from those used for the United States. In particular, output originating in government and in the stock of houses is included in the German aggregate, and the associated capital goods, houses, and employment are counted as inputs. Otherwise, the procedure is basically the same.

Table 2 is arranged like Table 1 except that it reports separately the estimates of the elasticities both when they are not constrained to add up to unity and when they are. The unconstrained elasticities add up to about 1.2 or 1.25; if they are taken at face value, then, the German economy was subject to substantial increasing returns to scale. Experience suggests that the same would have occurred if I had estimated similar unconstrained production functions for the United States. I have some reasons for not taking these results at face value. But actually I need not rely on those

Table 2

λ Rate of increase of productivity of capital	α Elasticity of output with respect to capital		$1-\alpha$ Elasticity of output with respect to labor		R^2
Constant Returns to Scale Not Imposed					
.00	2.2090	(.6969)	— 1.8170	(.7923)	.3322
.02	1.0404	(.1305)	0.0931	(.1466)	.8575
.03	0.7257	(.1196)	0.4748	(.1886)	.7294
.04	0.5647	(.0437)	0.6814	(.0889)	.8409
.05	0.4567	(.0652)	0.8089	(.1640)	.8082
Constant Returns to Scale Imposed					
.00	2.6668	(.5577)	— 1.6668		.8686
.02	0.9673	(.0462)	0.0327		.9880
.03	0.6685	(.0322)	0.3315		.9880
.04	0.5095	(.0259)	0.4905		.9861
.05	0.4116	(.0219)	0.5884		.9853

suspicions. It is remarkable that the estimates of the elasticity of potential output with respect to effective capital are very similar in the two halves of Table 2. This means that the implied estimates of the marginal productivity of effective capital are about the same whether or not there are constant returns to scale.

When Table 1 and the second half of Table 2 are compared, it appears that they are in a definite relationship to one another. For every rate of technical progress, the elasticities for the United States are approximately the same as the elasticities for Germany with a rate of technical progress one percentage point higher. Thus, when the rate of increase of the productivity of new capital is .02 in the U.S., the elasticity of output with respect to effective capital is 0.63; when λ for Germany is .03, α is .67. When λ in the United States is .03, α is .51; when λ for Germany is .04, α is .51. When λ for the United States is .04, α is .42; when λ for Germany is .05, α is .41. One is tempted to conclude from this that either the elasticities are the same in the two countries and the rate of technical progress one point higher in Germany, or that the rate of progress is the same in the two countries but the effective-capital-elasticity is higher in Germany by about .1. It is not necessarily the case that either of these things is true. There are two obstacles to any sharp conclusion, even if the validity of the model is not questioned: one is that the output and capital concepts differ for the two analyses; the other is that we have no very good criterion for choosing one of a range of equally acceptable values of λ. The only criterion there is comes from the notion that the capital elasticity should be about the same as the share of capital in income and output. For the U.S. this leads us to an α between .3 and .4 and a λ between .04 and .06. During the period in question, the share of wages in the national income of the German economy has been somewhat lower than in the United States. Thus in 1936 the compensation of employees was 55.4 per cent of national income in Western Germany and 66.1 per cent in the United States; in 1950 the figures were 60.8 and 64.3 per cent; in 1955, 63.6 and 68.9 per cent.

This comparison has some treacherous aspects, apart from the fact that the upward trend in the wage share in Germany casts doubt on the appropriateness of any Cobb-Douglas model. Recorded relative shares may be sensitive both to the proportion of economic activity carried on in unincorporated enterprises and to changes in that proportion, as well as to purely statistical differences. Still, if this kind of evidence suggests anything, it suggests that a value of α higher than the American one by 5 or 10 percentage points may be appropriate and, therefore, that the rates of technological progress may be about the same in the two countries. It is important to realize that this tentative hypothesis would not fly in the face of the obviously more rapid increase in man-hour productivity in Germany and in continental Europe generally. The rate of technical progress we are talking is the rate at which the intrinsic productivity of new capital rises. Overall productivity increases depend also on the rate at which capital is deepened, and the extent to which a high rate of investment modernizes the capital stock.

There is also room for different *levels* of technology in the two countries, even if rates of change are approximately the same. Such a difference is actually suggested by the data, as you will see. It stems in part from the different definitions of output and capital and in part, no doubt, from the richer natural resource endowment and higher educational level of the United States, and perhaps from the bigger scale of the economy.

It is quite possible that I ought to have treated the pre-war and post-war periods in Germany quite separately, to take account both of territorial changes and the bottleneck phenomena of the early postwar years. But that would have left me with time periods too short for my purposes. One can't in any case, speak of the 1925—1957 period as a whole. For 1925—1938, full employment GNP in Germany increased at an average annual rate between $3^1/_2$ and 4 per cent. One can guess roughly that a 5 per cent improvement in the productivity of new capital contributed about $2^1/_4$ per cent a year to the growth of output; the supply of labor increased at 0.8 per cent a year and contributed perhaps a half of one per cent a year to the growth of GNP; the conventional capital stock grew at 1.4 per cent a year and contributed about three-quarters of one per cent to the annual growth of output. In 1950—1957, the effective stock of capital grew at a rate in excess of 10 per cent a year and accounts for perhaps 5.8 per cent a year growth in output; employment grew at 2.2 per cent annually, and explains another 1.5 per cent annual growth. Output grew at about 7.8 per cent a year, and the long-run production function does not account for the extra half of one per cent a year.

A Comparison of Rates of Return

According to a formula given in the preceding lecture, the

social rate of return on investment in this model is equal to the marginal product of effective capital minus an allowance for depreciation and for obsolescence. That formula holds for the year zero, but I can always renumber the years so that 1954 is the year zero. Remembering that Q stands for potential output and J the effective stock of capital, the formula for the rate of return can be written $r = \alpha \; Q/J - (\lambda + d)/(1 + \lambda)$ where α is the elasticity of output with respect to capital, λ the rate of technical progress, and d the depreciation rate.

In this context, the appropriate depreciation rate refers entirely to physical wear and tear. Obsolescence is taken care of elsewhere in the model. Thus the average length of life will be longer (and d smaller) than we are used to in private profit calculations. The series for effective capital in the United States was constructed with a survival table that implies an average life of 17—20 years for equipment and about 50 years for plant. The source of the German data suggests a life of about 25 years for equipment and all but plus infinity for buildings. It would seem that a depreciation rate of about 4 per cent is the right order of magnitude. Following the sources literally would suggest a slightly higher depreciation rate for the U.S., but differences of one percentage point are obviously insignificant in this kind of analysis.

Table 3 exhibits the raw materials for calculating the 1954 rate of return on investment in the U.S. and Germany. I have listed the buildings and equipment figures separately to re-emphasize an important fact. The particular figures I have used for the U.S. exclude houses from the stock of capital and the services derived from houses from output, while the German figures include both. This would not be very important except that the provision of shelter is not only an extraordinarily capital-intensive economic activity, but is also carried on in the United States, and possibly elsewhere, at an extremely low rate of return. It is not hard to explain this differential, but that is not my purpose. What does matter to me is that the treatment of housing means that any comparison of rates of return will be biased in favor of the United States, perhaps considerably, by virtue of the exclusion of this segment of economic activity. The only correct way to allow for this discrepancy would be to do the whole analysis on the same basis for both countries. It is not enough to add or subtract a rough estimate of the stock of houses and public buildings at the last step of the computations, because with them included the whole system of estimates might be different. If I must content myself with that kind of procedure it is only because I have not had time to do more.

I should make one other comment on Table 3. The rates of return computed from it are excessively high because inventories are not included in the capital figures. In the United States stocks amount to about a fifth of the annual GNP and this is enough to make a difference of about 5 percentage points in the rate of return. But the effect would be approximately the same in both countries and not so important to a comparison of rates of return.

I am now in an awkward position. Table 3 seems to show that the rates of return in 1954 were very similar in the two countries, and that if there was any systematic difference between them, the return on investment was higher in the United States. Yet I suspect that the contrary may have been true, and that my numerical results are compatible with that belief. I have already mentioned what I think is the most important bias in these figures, the inclusion of housing in

Table 3

Calculation of Rate of Return

United States 1954					
Rate of technical progress (λ)	.00	.02	.03	.04	.05
Potential Output (Q)	302	302	302	302	302
Effective Capital (J)	543	412	369	338	309
Effective Equipment	274	238	224	211	198
Effective Plant	270	175	145	127	111
Output per unit of Effective Capital (Q/J)	0.56	0.73	0.82	0.89	0.98
Estimated α	1.24	0.63	0.51	0.42	0.36
α Q/J	0.69	0.46	0.43	0.37	0.35
Depreciation and obsolescence $(d + \lambda)/(1 + \lambda)$	.04	.06	.07	.08	.09
Rate of Return	0.65	0.40	0.36	0.29	0.26

Germany 1954					
Rate of technical progress (λ)	.00	.02	.03	.04	.05
Potential Output (Q)	154	154	154	154	154
Effective Capital (J)	614	327	275	235	214
Effective Equipment	180	135	123	111	104
Effective Buildings	434	193	152	124	110
Output per unit of Effective Capital (Q/J)	0.25	0.46	0.56	0.66	0.72
Estimated α	2.67	0.97	0.67	0.51	0.41
α Q/J	0.67	0.45	0.38	0.34	0.30
Depreciation and obsolescence	.04	.06	.07	.08	.09
Rate of Return	0.63	0.39	0.31	0.26	0.21

the German data and its exclusion in the American data. The source of the paradox is evident enough: the data show the average product of capital to be higher in the United States than in Germany by more than enough to compensate for the higher elasticity of output with respect to capital in Germany. Of course this is not logically inconsistent with the notion that the United States is a much more capital-intensive economy than the German. That notion seems to correspond to the facts. In 1954, equipment per worker was about twice as great in the U.S. as in Germany. It could be, as I have mentioned before, that the production function for the United States is so much higher than that for Germany that even at higher degrees of capital-intensiveness the return to investment is higher. In view of the resource endowment, the diffusion of education, and the size of the American economy this would not be very implausible.

But I think there is a simpler explanation. The column in Table 3 marked $\lambda = 0$, contains conventional capital stock measures. In 1954, the stock of plant and equipment in the United States was divided almost evenly between plant and equipment. The proportion between buildings and machinery has been changing over time; in 1929 the stock of buildings was about $1^1/_2$ times the stock of equipment. In Germany, however, the stock of buildings was almost $2^1/_2$ times the stock of equipment in 1954, and more than 3 times as large in 1929. There is no reason why the proportions between plant and equipment should be the same in two countries with different climates and different mixtures of industries. But clearly most of the difference must represent houses.

In the United States, currently, the stock of houses is about

40 per cent of the total stock of reproducible capital, *i.e.* about $2/3$ as big as the stock of plant and equipment. A rough estimate of the stock of plant, equipment, and houses is therefore $ 800 billion, of which $ 630 billion would be buildings. This would make the ratio of buildings to equipment about $2^1/3$ to 1, not far from the German figure. Correspondingly, I must increase the measure of output to include the services of houses. This adds under 10 per cent to potential output. The net result is an average product of capital of about $ 330 $\div$ 800, or about .4, much closer to the German figure of .26. Even thus adjusted, output per unit of capital is higher in Germany than in the United States, and I take this to be testimony in favor of the hypothesis that the level of technology, if not its rate of change, is substantially higher in the United States.

Unfortunately, I can not by such simple devices put the 'effective stock' figures on a comparable basis. It is clear, however, that the same systematic bias is present. Notice, for example, that while output per unit of effective capital, with $\lambda = .05$, was .98 in the U.S. and .72 in Germany, output per unit of effective equipment was 1.53 in the U.S. and 1.48, almost the same, in Germany.

After my rough correction for houses, the buildings-equipment ratio appeared to be about the same in 1954 in the two countries. It is perhaps as good an assumption as any other that 'effective buildings' and 'effective equipment' bore the same ratio to one another in the U.S. and in Germany. In that case the effective stock of capital (with a 5 per cent rate of improvement) in the United States, houses included, would be something over $ 400 billion. Output per unit of effective capital would be corrected to about .74. With $\alpha = .36$, the gross marginal product of effective capital would be something like 27 per cent, and the net rate of return about 18 per cent per year.

These rough adjustments have little to recommend them except that they are easily made. Yet even after they are performed they suggest social rates of return to investment in 1954 of 21 per cent a year in Germany and 18 per cent a year in the United States. Clearly all that one can say—and this comes as a surprise to me—is that the social return to investment was approximately the same in the United States and Germany in the mid-1950's.

If similar calculations are made for the year 1957 (which is as far as the German data extend), the results are quite interesting. Corresponding to Table 3 (with $\lambda = .05$), I find a rate of return of 23—25 per cent a year in the U.S., and about 19 per cent in Germany. So there is some evidence of of a falling rate of return. The implication is that the deepening of capital has proceeded sufficiently rapidly that it is not fully offset by technological progress. This is an important conclusion if it could be verified, and I will return to it shortly.

Comparison between the United States and Germany in 1957 are as difficult as in 1954, because of the difference in definitions. The best I can do is to make the same crude adjustment as for 1954: add to the effective stock of plant in the United States an amount large enough to make the ratio of effective plant to effective equipment the same in the two countries. There is some justification for this in the fact that output per unit of effective equipment is almost the same in the two countries. If that adjustment is made, then my estimate of the rate of return in the United States falls to 16—17 per cent. I am left with the very shaky impression that the social rate of return is not very different in the two countries, and with only the slightest support for my *a priori* belief that it is likely to be lower in the United States than in Germany.

Tentative Conclusions

One conclusion you will have leaped to yourself. It is a very tricky and delicate business to learn something about the social return to investment, and I have raised more questions than I have answered. In a way that is all to the good. One of the objects of the de Vries lectures is to provide 'a stimulus to theoretical work in economics in the Netherlands', as if that were needed. But Dutch economists have with few exceptions shied away from capital theory, both pure and applied. Maybe what the subject needs is a dose of Dutch down-to-earth theorizing and practical ingenuity. If I have got you interested in the problem I will have done more to solve it than I had hoped.

A second conclusion stems from the suggestion in the figures that the social profitability of investment fell between 1954 and 1957.* Suppose that private profitability tends to change over time in the same direction as social profitability. This seems likely to be so. Then perhaps the so-called 'profit

---

* In the U.S., the data suggest little or no change in the social rate of return between 1957 and 1960. In view of the well-known weakness of fixed investment during those years, this finding is consistent with my interpretation.

squeeze' of recent years, both in Germany and the United States, is a more fundamental economic phenomenon than many commentators have thought. It seems clear to me that much of what is called a profit squeeze in the United States is simply a reflection of inadequate effective demand and resulting excess capacity. But it may well be that even a return to high levels of economic activity would not succeed in putting profit rates up to their level during the early postwar period, for good oldfashioned diminishing-returns reasons. In that case, an economic policy which is designed to promote growth through private investment has a difficult task before it, and it remains to be seen whether conventional monetary-fiscal methods are adequate. I must say that my colleague Paul Samuelson had already come to this same conclusion by his own subtle methods. That my crude figures lead to the same result as Samuelson's educated intuition gives me hope for econometric methods.

The apparent fall in profit rates in Germany can hardly be the consequence of weakness in overall demand. Nor do I think it very satisfactory to attribute it to some sudden militancy in the trade union movement. If the social profitability of investment was falling even before 1957 because of the rapid accumulation of capital, then one would surely except it to be falling more sharply now that surplus labor has been absorbed and the flow of refugees from the East has stopped. In that case both the squeeze on private profits and the activism of the trade unions may be reflecting a fundamental shift in the relative scarcity of capital and labor.

My third conclusion is a negative one. As I have already confessed, I had expected to find a lower social rate of return in the United States than in Germany. Instead I have drawn a blank. After some doctoring of the figures I was able to extract a hint that perhaps the social return to fixed capital investment was after all a trifle lower in the United States. But of course all that one can honestly say is that whatever the difference in rates of return may be, it is so small as to be swamped by the crudenesses and incomparabilities of the data and the excessively simple character of the model. By the way, estimating rates of return on investment has become a popular indoor sport at M.I.T., surpassing even Three-Stage Least Squares. My colleagues Richard Eckaus and Louis Lefeber have devised their own scheme for playing the game, which is related to, but not exactly like, mine. They do not pay explicit attention to technical progress but they use shorter periods of time and so presumably it does not matter very much. Their estimate of the social rate of return in the United States around 1954—57 is 18—20 per cent, compared to my figure of 19—26 per cent. Eckaus and Lefeber have also made estimates for the Netherlands in the mid-1950's and they come out in the neighborhood of 15—22 per cent. Thus their findings are compatible with the proposition that differences among advanced countries in the rate of return on investment are slight, and in particular that the rate of return is not radically lower in the United States than in some European countries. I have already mentioned some reasons why this could be true despite the higher ratio of capital to labor (but not necessarily to natural resources) in the United States. But one can't get too excited over economists' ability to rationalize, after the fact, whatever they happen to observe.

Fourth, I would like to call your attention to the fact that all the social rates of return we have talked about are in the 15—20 per cent per year range, and perhaps even higher if we neglect housing and think mainly of business investment. I think these are surprisingly high figures. If they are anywhere near right, then they suggest that rates of investment considerably higher than the current ones might be socially desirable. In the United States, many people save voluntarily to buy riskless assets paying 4 or 5 per cent annual interest. Presumably, then, large classes of people have a marginal rate of time preference no greater than 4 or 5 per cent a year. Of course, single productive investments are far from riskless, even apart from the danger of cyclical recession which is still real in the United States. But a large number of investments taken together carry a greatly reduced risk per dollar, if only they have some statistical independence, and the main requirement for that is that the business cycle not be too severe. If the whole economy can be thought of as a bank capable of paying 15—20 per cent interest, then it would seem to be in society's interest to find ways of making somewhat larger deposits.

This leads me to a fifth and last conclusion. The social rates of return I have calculated seem to be high not only relative to the interest rates at which individuals evince a willingness to save, but high also compared with *ex post* private rates of profit. For the United States in 1957, Denison has estimated a private rate of return on non-agricultural, non-residential private capital of something like 13 per cent a year. With agriculture included, the rate would be a little lower. On the other hand rates nearer 20 per cent are not unrepresentative of the 'target' rates of return *ex ante* at which industry seems to aim. This suggests that if the social return to investment in durable capital does exceed the private return and if the market can therefore be expected to under-invest, one source of the discrepancy may lie in the divergence between private and social risk. In the United States the risk of cyclical underutilization may be in turn the main component of private risk. If that is so, then an effective full-employment policy could reduce the discrepancy and, by stimulating the demand for private investment, lead both to more rapid economic growth and more effective allocation of resources. Beyond that, tax policy might aim at further 'socialization of risk' by making the Treasury a greater partner in losses as well as profits.

A Final Word

Professor de Vries, in whose name these lectures exist, once described economic theory as a storeroom of thoughts. I suppose it is also a storeroom of errors. I am under no illusion that I have avoided adding a few errors to the contents of the storeroom. But part of the job of economics is weeding out errors. That is much harder than making them, but also more fun.

Rotterdam, May, 1963.

References

ARROW, KENNETH J., The Economic Implications of Learning by Doing, Review of Economic Studies, pp. 155—173, June 1962.

CHAMPERNOWNE, D. G., A Dynamic Growth Model Including a Production Function, in The Theory of Capital (ed. F. A. Lutz and D. C. Hague), pp. 223—244, Macmillan 1961.

ECKAUS R. S., and LOUIS LEFEBER, Capital Formation: A Theoretical and Empirical Analysis, Review of Economics and Statistics, pp. 113—122, May 1962.

KOYCK L. M., and Mrs. M. J. 't HOOFT-WELVAARS, Economic Growth, Marginal Productivity of Capital and the Rate of Interest, to be published in the proceedings of the International Economics Association conference on The Rate of Interest, Royaumont, 1962.

PHELPS, E.S., The New View of Investment: A Neoclassical Analysis, Quarterly Journal of Economics, pp. 548—567, Nov. 1962.

SAMUELSON, P. A., Parable and Realism in Capital Theory: The Surrogate Production Function, Review of Economic Studies, pp. 193—206, June 1962.

SOLOW, R. M., Investment and Technical Progress, in Mathematical Methods in the Social Sciences 1959 (ed. K. J. Arrow, S. Karlin and P. Suppes), pp. 89—104, Stanford University Press, 1960.
Technical Progress, Capital Formation and Economic Growth, American Economic Review, pp. 76—86, May 1962.

TOBIN, JAMES, Money, Capital and Other Stores of Value, American Economic Review, pp. 26—37, May 1961.

WORSWICK, G. D. N., Mrs. Robinson on Simple Accumulation, Oxford Economic Papers, pp. 125—142, June 1959.